PUFFIN BOOKS

NINE O'CLOCK BELL

Whatever you think about school, you're sure to find lots to entertain and amuse in this enjoyable and lively collection of poetry.

Nine o'Clock Bell contains more than a hundred poems, all of them in one way or another about school – getting ready for it, going to it, liking it, hating it and even playing truant from it! Best friends and bullies, teachers and homework, fights in the playground, mucking about in the classroom; almost every aspect of school life, past and present, can be found in this anthology. The list of poets is equally wide-ranging and you can find poems by Walter de la Mare, Roger McGough, D. H. Lawrence, Charles Causley, John Betjeman, Michael Rosen and many others. Whether sad, funny or just interesting, the host of characters to be found in *Nine o'Clock Bell* are as memorable and realistic as those in any school classroom.

Raymond Wilson is Professor of Education at Reading University, and as well as being an established poet himself, has worked on children's poetry and prose for over twenty years.

Nine o'Clock Bell

Poems about School

Chosen by Raymond Wilson

Illustrated by Jon Riley

PUFFIN BOOKS

Puffin Books, Penguin Books Ltd, Harmondsworth, Middlesex, England
Viking Penguin Inc., 40 West 23rd Street, New York, New York 10010, U.S.A.
Penguin Books Australia Ltd, Ringwood, Victoria, Australia
Penguin books Canada Ltd, 2801 John Street, Markham, Ontario, Canada L3R 1B4
Penguin books (N.Z.) Ltd, 182–190 Wairau Road, Auckland 10, New Zealand

First published by Viking Kestrel 1985
Published in Puffin Books 1987

Made and printed in Great Britain by
Richard Clay Ltd, Bungay, Suffolk
Typeset in Baskerville

Contents

Getting Ready for School

Kate, Kate,
I know you'll be late!
Here is your satchel and here is your slate.
Don't go like that, child, your hair's in a state –
Kate! Kate! Kate!

Kate, Kate,
It's twenty to nine,
Take your umbrella, it may not be fine.
Oh, what a hanky – you'd better take mine –
Kate! Kate! Kate!

Kate, Kate,
You haven't your fare!
Here are your sandwiches on the hall chair.
What's that? – your hockey stick – where, darling, where?
Kate! Kate! Kate!

Kate, Kate,
Your gym shoes are here,
Won't you be needing your pencil-box, dear?
Try to speak slower, love, Mother can't hear –
Kate! Kate! Kate!

Kate, Kate,
You'd better not wait,
The two little Smith girls have just passed the gate.
Hurry up, darling, I know you'll be late –
Kate! Kate! Kate!

Caryl Brahms

The False Knight upon the Road

'O where are you going?'
Quoth the false knight upon the road:
'I'm going to school.'
Quoth the wee boy, and still he stood.

'What is that upon your back?'
Quoth the false knight upon the road:
'Why, sure it is my books.'
Quoth the wee boy, and still he stood.

'What is that you've got in your arm?'
Quoth the false knight upon the road:
'Why sure it is my peat.' [1]
Quoth the wee boy, and still he stood.

'Whose are those sheep?'
Quoth the false knight upon the road:
'They're mine and my mother's.'
Quoth the wee boy, and still he stood.

'How many of them are mine?'
Quoth the false knight upon the road:
'All them that have blue tails.'
Quoth the wee boy, and still he stood.

'I wish you were on yon tree.'
Quoth the false knight upon the road:
'And a good ladder under me.'
Quoth the wee boy, and still he stood.

1. Peat for the school fire.

'And the ladder for to break.'
Quoth the false knight upon the road:
'And *you* for to fall down.'
Quoth the wee boy, and still he stood.

'I wish you were in yon sea.'
Quoth the false knight upon the road:
'And a good boat under me.'
Quoth the wee boy, and still he stood.

'And the boat for to break.'
Quoth the false knight upon the road:
'And *you* to be drowned.'
Quoth the wee boy, and still he stood.

Unknown

The Schoolboy

I love to rise in a summer morn
When the birds sing on every tree;
The distant huntsman winds his horn,
And the sky-lark sings with me.
O! what sweet company.

But to go to school in a summer morn,
O! it drives all joy away;
Under a cruel eye outworn,
The little ones spend the day
In sighing and dismay.

Ah! then at times I drooping sit,
And spend many an anxious hour,
Nor in my book can I take delight,
Nor sit in learning's bower,
Worn through with the dreary shower.

How can the bird that is born for joy
Sit in a cage and sing?
How can a child, when fears annoy,
But droop his tender wing,
And forget his youthful spring?

O! father and mother, if buds are nipped
And blossoms blown away,
And if the tender plants are stripped
Of their joy in the springing day,
By sorrow and care's dismay,

How shall the summer arise in joy,
Or the summer fruits appear?
Or how shall we gather what griefs destroy,
Or bless the mellowing year,
When the blasts of winter appear?

William Blake

I've Got an Apple Ready

My hair's tightly plaited;
I've a bright blue bow;
I don't want my breakfast,
And now I must go.

My satchel's on my shoulder;
Nothing's out of place;
And I've got an apple ready,
Just in case.

So it's 'Good-bye Mother!'
And off down the street;
Briskly at first
On pit-a-pat feet,

But slow and more slow
As I reach the tarred
Trackway that runs
By Hodson's Yard;

For it's there sometimes
Bill Craddock waits for me
To snatch off my beret
And throw it in a tree.

Bill Craddock leaning
On Hodson's rails;
Bill with thin hands
And dirty nails;

Bill with a front tooth
Broken and bad;
His dark eyes cruel,
And somehow sad.

Often there are workmen,
And then he doesn't dare;
But this morning I feel
He'll be there.

At the corner he will pounce . . .
But quickly I'll say
'Hallo, Bill! have an apple!' –
In an ordinary way.

I'll push it in his hand
And walk right on;
And when I'm round the corner
I'll run!

John Walsh

Bus to School

Rounding the corner
It comes to a stay.
Quick! Grab a rail!
Now we're off on our way . . .
Oh, but it's Thursday,
The day of fear!
Three hateful lessons!
And school draws near.

Here in the bus though
There's plenty to see:
Boys full of talk about
Last night's TV;
Girls with their violins,
Armfuls of twigs
And flowers for teacher;
Bartlett and Biggs;
Conductor who chats with them,
Jokes about cricket;
Machine that flicks out
A white ribbon of ticket . . .
Yes, but it's Thursday,
The day of fear! –
Six hateful lessons!
And school draws near.

Conductor now waiting,
Firm as a rock,
For Billy whose penny's
Slid down in his sock.
Conductor frowning,
Hand on his handle;

Poor Billy blushes,
Undoes his sandal . . .
'Hold very tight, please,
Any more fares?'
Whistling conductor
Goes clumping upstairs . . .
Boots up above now!
Boys coming down! . . .
Over the hump-bridge
And into the town.

Old Warren sweeping
In his shirt-sleeves!
Sun on his shop-front,
Sun on the leaves . . .
Only, it's Thursday,
The day of fear!
All hateful lessons!
And school draws near.

John Walsh

Animal Chatter
a piece of doggerel

The other morning, feeling dog-tired, I was walking
    sluggishly to school,
When I happened upon two girls I know – who were busy
    playing the fool.

They were monkeying about, having a fight –
But all that they said didn't sound quite right.
'You're batty, you are – and you're catty too.'
'That's better than being ratty, you peevish shrew!'
'Don't be so waspish!' 'Don't be such a pig!'
'Look who's getting cocky – your head's too big!'
'You silly goose! Let me have my say!'
'Why should I, you elephantine popinjay?!'
I stopped, I looked, I listened – and I had to laugh
Because I realized then, of course, it's never the cow or
   the calf
That behave in this bovine way.
It's mulish humans like those girls I met the other day.
You may think I'm too dogged, but something fishy's
   going on –
The way we beastly people speak of animals is definitely
   wrong.
Crabs are rarely crabby and mice are never mousey
(And I believe all lice deny that they are lousy.)
You know, if I wasn't so sheepish and if I had my way
I'd report the English language to the RSPCA.

Gyles Brandreth

School Bell

Nine o'Clock Bell!
Nine o'Clock Bell!
All the small children and big ones as well,
Pulling their stockings up, snatching their hats,
Checking and grumbling and giving back-chats,
Laughing and quarrelling, dropping their things,
These at a snail's pace and those upon wings,
Lagging behind a bit, running ahead,
Waiting at corners for lights to turn red,
Some of them scurrying,
Others not worrying,
Carelessly trudging or anxiously hurrying,
All through the streets they are coming pell-mell
At the Nine o'Clock
Nine o'Clock
Nine o'Clock
Bell!

Eleanor Farjeon

School

Schoolboys scamper with smiling shining faces.
Girls in groups gape and gossip at the gate.
Nervous knots of newcomers.
Big books bulge in brown bags.
Car doors clash and clank and clatter.
Bells bring boys bustling, banging, bothering, bouncing.
Girls go grumbling and groaning along gangways.
Action at Assembly.
Crowds come clamouring into classrooms.
Girls go and group for games.
Boys battle bravely with boredom.
In Maths some mutter in misery.
Slowly silence settles in school.
Bells bleat for dinner-break.
Great the galloping and gallumphing.
Grace ungracefully groaned.
Scrumptious sizzling sausages sighing to be swallowed.
Slurping and sloshing and slopping.
Great guzzling and greedy galloping.

Janet, Paul and Christine
aged 12

Not Guilty

We have assembly every day
Assembly in the hall
And every day (or so it seems)
The Head, who's ten feet tall
(Or so it seems), has lots to say
About the writing on the wall.
And (so it seems) just every day
He looks at me with marbled eye
And makes me feel I wrote it all.
I go quite red from head to foot
(Or so it seems) and try to stare
Right back at him.
     'How do you dare,'
I want to shout, 'to make me feel
I wrote that stuff?' I'm more the type
Who'd look for rags to wipe
It out (or so it seems).

John Kitching

A Lapp at School in Finland

He went away to school
willingly enough

But he soon came to regret it
At school they spoke a strange language
and there was no trout-lake near
If you felt like fishing
you had to slip out to a pond
and fish for strange little fish with red eyes

He missed the fells
He was almost smothered by the pines
He felt more and more out of place

He wet his bed at night
He would hide in the hayloft to weep
in secret

*

He came to live in the boarding-school
He had never seen such a big building
He was afraid of getting lost in it

The school matron was broader than she was tall
Her breasts were like cushions
which swung as she walked
The matron was nasty
she often made him
stand as a punishment
hold up his hands
level with his shoulders
with stone-chips on his fingers

If the stones fell off
you got birched on the nails

The little stones kept falling off

*

One day
in their school they were taught
about minorities
about primitive peoples
who can be found
in our country too
and who are called
Lapps

He felt
the others looking
he heard

*

So anyway that autumn came
The leaves fell from the trees
The ground grew bare
The wind sighed
swept up the scattered leaves
and in the open the birds' merriment was heard no more

One morning the blades of grass and
the dwarf birches were covered in rime
the birches bristled under the strain of the ice
The little autumn birds fluttered in flocks
from dwarf birch to dwarf birch
they twittered a moment and flew off again

The sky was blue
The sun shed its beams
like grains between the fingers
it spread a fleeting warmth
Sounds dwindled
Nature waited

He was alone
The rapids roared
There was no more school
it was autumn

Nils-Aslak Valkeapää
translated from the Lapp by
Hannele Branch and Keith Bosley

The Lesson

A poem that raises the question:
Should there be capital punishment in schools?

Chaos ruled O K in the classroom
as bravely the teacher walked in
the nooligans ignored him
his voice was lost in the din

'The theme for today is violence
and homework will be set
I'm going to teach you a lesson
one that you'll never forget'

He picked on a boy who was shouting
and throttled him then and there
then garotted the girl behind him
(the one with grotty hair)

Then sword in hand he hacked his way
between the chattering rows
'First come, first severed' he declared
'fingers, feet, or toes'

He threw the sword at a latecomer
it struck with deadly aim
then pulling out a shotgun
he continued with his game

The first blast cleared the backrow
(where those who skive hang out)
they collapsed like rubber dinghies
when the plug's pulled out

'Please may I leave the room sir?'
a trembling vandal enquired
'Of course you may' said teacher
put the gun to his temple and fired

The Head popped a head round the doorway
to see why a din was being made
nodded understandingly
then tossed in a grenade

And when the ammo was well spent
with blood on every chair
Silence shuffled forward
with its hands up in the air

The teacher surveyed the carnage
the dying and the dead
He waggled a finger severely
'Now let that be a lesson' he said

Roger McGough

Arithmetic

Arithmetic is where numbers fly like pigeons in and out
   of your head.
Arithmetic tells you how many you lose or win if you
   know how many you had before you lost or won.

Arithmetic is seven eleven all good children go to heaven
   – or five six bundle of sticks.
Arithmetic is numbers you squeeze from your head to your
   hand to your pencil to your paper till you get the
   answer.

Arithmetic is where the answer is right and everything is
  nice and you can look out of the window and see the
  blue sky – or the answer is wrong and you have to start
  all over again and try again and see if it comes out this
  time.
If you take a number and double it and double it again
  and then double it a few more times, the number gets
  bigger and bigger and goes higher and higher and
  only arithmetic can tell you what the number is when
  you decide to quit doubling.
Arithmetic is where you have to multiply – and you carry
  the multiplication table in your head and hope you
  won't lose it.
If you have two animal crackers, one good and one bad,
  and you eat one and a striped zebra with streaks all
  over him eats the other, how many animal crackers will
  you have if somebody offers you five six seven and you
  say No no no and you say Nay nay nay and you say
  Nix nix nix?
If you ask your mother for one fried egg for breakfast and
  she gives you two fried eggs and you eat both of them,
  who is better in arithmetic, you or your mother?

Carl Sandburg

Multiplication

Multiplication is vexation,
Division is as bad;
The Rule of Three it puzzles me,
And Fractions drive me mad.

Benjamin Franklin

Patterns

The other side of learning is forgetting.
How can you open your eyes if they don't close?
Teachers find this very upsetting.
They like you to be always on your toes.

Anybody can see that x equals y
When it's written in white chalk on a black wall.
Just as anyone can see that a black cloud in a blue sky
Means that rain is going to fall.

Tidy children are good, untidy children are slatterns.
Everything is labelled according to looks.
But beneath our lids spring rainbow-coloured patterns
That were never found in books.

Olive Dehn

The Nature Lesson

The teacher has the flowers on her desk,
Then goes round, giving one to each of us.
We are going to study the primrose –
To find out all about it. It has five petals,
Notice the little dent in each, making it heart-shaped
And a pale green calyx (And O! the hairy stem!).
Now, in the middle of the flower
There may be a little knob – that is the pistil –
Or perhaps your flower may show the bunch of stamens.
        We look at our flowers
To find out which kind we have got.

Now we are going to look inside,
So pull your petals off, one by one.
        But wait . . .
If I pull my flower to pieces it will stop
Being a primrose. It will be just bits
Strewn on my desk. I can't pull it to pieces.
What does it matter what goes on inside?
I won't find out by pulling it to pieces,
Because it will not be a primrose any more,
And the bits will not mean anything at all.
A primrose is a primrose, not just bits.

It lies there, a five-petalled primrose,
A whole primrose, a living primrose.
To find out what is inside I make it dead,
And then it will not be a primrose.
        You can't find out
What goes on inside a living flower that way.
The teacher talks, fingers rustle . . .
I will look over my neighbour's flower
And leave my primrose whole. But if the teacher comes

And tells me singly to pull my flower to pieces
Then I will do as I am told. The teacher comes,
Passes my neighbour on her gangway side,
Does not see my primrose is still whole,
Goes by, not noticing; nobody notices.

My flower remains a primrose, that they all
Want to find out about by pulling to pieces.
I am alone: all the world is alone
In the flower left breathing on my desk.

Marjorie Baldwin

Wild Flowers

'Of what are you afraid, my child?'
   inquired the kindly teacher.
'Oh, sir! the flowers, they are wild,'
   replied the timid creature.

Peter Newell

Visit to a Graveyard

Last Tuesday, instead of just sitting at desks in school to
    slave hard,
Miss Richardson took her class 3C down to St Leonard's
    graveyard.
'It will give us something interesting,' she said, 'to write
    about for homework' –
A remark that caused among the boys and girls of 3C a
    certain amount of groanwork.
Still, they went. No bodies are planted there now and the
    church itself is all broken down and torn –
Which had Miss using quite a number of fancy words like
    'abandoned' and 'derelict' and 'forlorn'.

*

And 3C had a fine time:
    Grubbing round grassy graves,
    Trying to decipher names and dates,
    Tripping over kerbs,
    Finding green chippings deep in the grass,
    Picking blackberries,
And generally behaving quite well, Miss said.

*

She also said, 'A poem then, children.
Quite short,
With rhymes if you can.
And do try and capture the atmosphere.'

Neville's poem said:
>   That place is an almighty shambles,
>   I tore my trousers on the brambles.
>   My mum's furious; she says our teacher
>   Must be a proper crazy creature.

Peter said:
>   In purple spray
>   On a gravestone grey
>   It says MAN UNITED.
>   Someone's a fool
>   'Cos the best is LIVERPOOL!

Julia wrote:
>   My dad says
>   In *his* schooldays
>   Kids got the birch hard
>   Not trips around some mucky churchyard.

And Podge wrote:
>   I didn't see no skellingtons,
>   And all dirt and grot
>   Got in me wellingtons.

*

'It's clear,' said their teacher, 'quite, quite clear
You just didn't feel the atmosphere.'

Eric Finney

Why English is so Hard

We'll begin with a box, and the plural is boxes;
But the plural of ox should be oxen, not oxes.
Then one fowl is goose, but two are called geese;
Yet the plural of moose should never be meese.
You may find a lone mouse or a whole lot of mice,
But the plural of house is houses, not hice.
If the plural of man is always called men,
Why shouldn't the plural of pan be called pen?
The cow in the plural may be cows or kine.
But the plural of vow is vows, not vine.
And I speak of a foot, and you show me your feet,
But I give you a boot – would a pair be called beet?
If one is a tooth and a whole set are teeth,
Why shouldn't the plural of booth be called beeth?
If the singular is this, and the plural is these,
Should the plural of kiss be nicknamed kese?
Then one may be that, and three may be those,
Yet the plural of hat would never be hose.
We speak of a brother, and also of brethren,
But though we say mother, we never say methren.

The masculine pronouns are he, his, and him,
But imagine the feminine she, shis, and shim!
So our English, I think you will all agree,
Is the trickiest language you ever did see.

Unknown

A History Lesson

Kings
like golden gleams
made with a mirror on the wall.

A non-alcoholic pope,
knights without arms,
arms without knights.

The dead like so many strained noodles,
a pound of those fallen in battle,
two ounces of those who were executed,

several heads
like so many potatoes
shaken into a cap —

empires rise and fall
at a wave of the pointer,
the blood is blotted out —

And only one small boy,
who was not paying the least attention,
will ask
between two victorious wars:

And did it hurt in those days too?

Miroslav Holub
translated from the Czech by
Ian Milner and George Theiner

Geography Lesson

When the jet sprang into the sky,
it was clear why the city
had developed the way it had,
seeing it scaled six inches to the mile.
There seemed an inevitability
about what on ground had looked haphazard,
unplanned and without style
when the jet sprang into the sky.

When the jet reached ten thousand feet,
it was clear why the country
had cities where rivers ran
and why the valleys were populated.
The logic of geography –
that land and water attracted man –
was clearly delineated
when the jet reached ten thousand feet.

When the jet rose six miles high,
it was clear that the earth was round
and that it had more sea than land.
But it was difficult to understand
that the men on the earth found
causes to hate each other, to build
walls across cities and to kill.
From that height, it was not clear why.

Zulfikar Ghose

Upright

I gazed enraptured
At the tide of children
Circling gaily and waving limbs
To the beat of the tambourine.

'Choose your gestures,'
The teacher's voice
Floated loud and clear
Above the barefoot din.

As by magic,
The children divided
Into those with bent backs
And those who crawled on fours.

Except for the odd one
Who stood his ground,
Looked to the left, looked to the right,
And preferred to remain upright.

Ada Aharoni

Holy Thursday

'Twas on a Holy Thursday, their innocent faces clean,
Came children walking two and two, in red, and blue,
  and green;
Grey headed beadles walked before, with wands as white
  as snow,
Till into the high dome of Paul's they like Thames' waters
  flow.

O what a multitude they seemed, these flowers of London
  town!
Seated in companies they sit with radiance all their own.
The hum of multitudes was there, but multitudes of
  lambs,
Thousands of little boys and girls raising their innocent
  hands.

Now like a mighty wind they raise to heaven the voice of
  song,
Or like harmonious thunderings the seats of heaven
  among.
Beneath them sit the aged men, wise guardians of the
  poor;
Then cherish pity, lest you drive an angel from your
  door.

William Blake

I'm a Treble in the Choir

In the Choir I'm a treble
And my singing is the debbel!
I'm a treble in the Choir!
They sing high but I sing higher.
Treble singing's VERY high,
But the highest high am I!
Soon I'll burst like any bubble:
I'm a treble – that's the trouble!

Edmond Kapp

Music Tutor

A tutor who taught on the flute
Tried to teach two young tooters to toot.
    Said the two to the tutor,
     'Is it harder to toot, or
To tutor two tooters to toot?'

Unknown

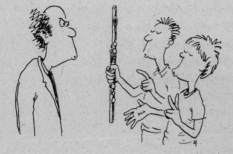

The High School Band

On warm days in September the high school band
Is up with the birds and marches along our street.
Boom boom.
To a field where it goes boom boom until eight forty-five
When it marches, as in the old rhyme, back, boom
    boom,
To its study halls, leaving our street
Empty except for the leaves that descend, to no drum,
And lie still.
In September
A great many high school bands beat a great many
    drums,
And the silences after their partings are very deep.

Reed Whittemore

Page of Handwriting

Two and two are four
four and four are eight
eight and eight are sixteen . . .
Again! says the teacher
Two and two are four
four and four are eight
eight and eight are sixteen.
But look the lyre-bird
flies by in the sky
the child sees it
the child hears it
the child calls it:
Save me
play with me
bird!
Then the bird comes down
and plays with the child
Two and two are four . . .
Again! says the teacher
and the child plays
the bird plays with him . . .
Four and four are eight
eight and eight are sixteen
and what are sixteen and sixteen?
Sixteen and sixteen are nothing
especially not thirty-two
anyway
and off they go.
And the child has hidden the bird
in his desk
and all the children
hear its song
and all the children

hear the music
and off go eight and eight in turn
and four and four and two and two
in turn push off
and one and one are neither one nor two
one and one go off as well.
And the lyre-bird plays
and the child sings
and the teacher shouts:
When you've all stopped fooling about!
But all the other children
are listening to the music
and the classroom walls
tumble calmly down.
And the windowpanes turn back into sand
the ink turns back into water
the desks turn back into trees
the chalk turns back into a cliff
the fountain-pen becomes a bird again.

Jacques Prévert
translated from the French by
Keith Bosley

Bird in the Classroom

The students drowsed and drowned
In the teacher's ponderous monotone –
Limp bodies looping in the wordy heat,
Melted and run together, desk and flesh as one,
Swooning and swimming in a sea of drone.

Each one asleep, swayed and vaguely drifted
With lidding eyes and lolling, weighted heads,
Was caught on heavy waves and dimly lifted,
Sunk slowly, ears ringing, in the syrup of his sound,
Or borne from the room on a heaving wilderness of beds.

And then, on a sudden, a bird's cool voice
Punched out song. Crisp and spare
On the startled air,
Beak-beamed
Or idly tossed,
Each note gleamed
Like a bead of frost.

A bird's cool voice from a neighbour tree
With five clear calls – mere grains of sound
Rare and neat
Repeated twice . . .
But they sprang the heat
Like drops of ice.

Ears cocked, before the comment ran
Fading and chuckling where a wattle stirred,
The students wondered how they could have heard
Such dreary monotones from man,
Such wisdom from a bird.

Colin Thiele

A Day in the Country

That summer Saturday they took us by coach
deep into the countryside, a sixty-mile journey,
told us how much we should enjoy it,
forty of us and four of our teachers.

Once off the motorway we were soon there,
a village with a tall spired church,
one street, thatched houses dotted here and there,
a public house and a shop where they sold
everything from stamps to pet food and bacon;
we bought ice creams there.

We ate our sandwiches on the vicar's lawn,
he gave us lemonade and strawberries,
and said we could go anywhere
but must shut all gates behind us.
I went with my teacher to the church,
marble monuments and flowers,
a Saxon font, box pews and a musty smell,
wandered around the overgrown graveyard,
reading the names and the dates on the tombs.

Then we all walked by the river,
saw some men and a heron fishing,
cows standing in the cool waters;
back through long fields of sheep
and a little wood loud with birds.

We played games in a daisied meadow,
got stung by wasps, chased by a bull,
and spoke to a farmer
who was just about to start milking.

But there was nothing to do,
I was bored with it all.

Before we left, some white-haired old ladies
gave us tea in a flowery garden,
bread and butter, milk and rock cakes,
asked us our names.

At last we crowded into the coach,
sang all the way home.

How glad we were to get back
to our noisy streets, to the shops we knew,
football, cinemas, the telly,
riding our bikes on the pavement,
fish and chips, Coca-Cola,
our homes towering into the sky,
father and mother coming in from work,
our friends of every colour.

They were kind to us in the village,
good to lie in the sun,
but one day was enough.
I should not like to live there,
everybody was so old
and there were only six children.

Leonard Clark

To David, about His Education

The world is full of mostly invisible things,
And there is no way but putting the mind's eye,
Or its nose, in a book, to find them out,
Things like the square root of Everest
Or how many times Byron goes into Texas,
Or whether the law of the excluded middle
Applies west of the Rockies. For these
And the like reasons, you have to go to school
And study books and listen to what you are told,
And sometimes try to remember. Though I don't know
What you will do with the mean annual rainfall
Of Plato's Republic, or the calorie content
Of the Diet of Worms, such things are said to be
Good for you, and you will have to learn them
In order to become one of the grown-ups
Who sees invisible things neither steadily nor whole,
But keeps gravely the grand confusion of the world
Under his hat, which is where it belongs,
And teaches small children to do this in their turn.

Howard Nemerov

My Son Asks Me

My young son asks me: Should I learn mathematics?
What for, I'm inclined to say. That two bits of bread are
   more than one
You'll notice anyway.
My young son asks me: Should I learn French?
What for, I'm inclined to say. That empire is going
   under.
Just rub your hand across your belly and groan
And you'll be understood all right.
My young son asks me: Should I learn history?
What for, I'm inclined to say. Learn to stick your head in
   the ground
Then maybe you'll come through.

Yes, learn mathematics, I tell him
Learn French, learn history!

Bertolt Brecht
translated from the German

What Did You Learn in School Today

What did you learn in school today,
Dear little boy of mine?
What did you learn in school today,
Dear little boy of mine?
I learned that Washington never told a lie,
I learned that soldiers seldom die,
I learned that everybody's free,
That's what the teacher said to me,
And that's what I learned in school today,
That's what I learned in school.

What did you learn in school today,
Dear little boy of mine?
What did you learn in school today,
Dear little boy of mine?
I learned that policemen are my friends,
I learned that justice never ends,
I learned that murderers die for their crimes,
Even if we make a mistake sometimes,
And that's what I learned in school today,
That's what I learned in school.

What did you learn in school today,
Dear little boy of mine?
What did you learn in school today,
Dear little boy of mine?
I learned our government must be strong,
It's always right and never wrong,
Our leaders are the finest men,
And we elect them again and again,
And that's what I learned in school today,
That's what I learned in school.

What did you learn in school today,
Dear little boy of mine?
What did you learn in school today,
Dear little boy of mine?
I learned that war is not so bad,
I learned about the great ones we have had,
We fought in Germany and in France,
And someday I might get my chance,
And that's what I learned in school today,
That's what I learned in school.

Tom Paxton

Lies

Telling lies to the young is wrong.
Proving to them that lies are true is wrong.
Telling them that God's in his heaven
and all's well with the world is wrong.
The young know what you mean. The young are people.
Tell them the difficulties can't be counted,
and let them see not only what will be
but see with clarity these present times.
Say obstacles exist they must encounter
sorrow happens, hardship happens.
The hell with it. Who never knew
the price of happiness will not be happy.
Forgive no error you recognize,
it will repeat itself, increase,
and afterwards our pupils
will not forgive in us what we forgave.

Yevgeny Yevtushenko
translated from the Russian by
Robin Milner-Gulland and Peter Levi

Our School

I go to Weld Park Primary,
It's near the Underpass
And five blocks past the Cemetery
And two roads past the Gas
Works with the big tower that smells so bad
    me and me mates put our hankies over our
        faces and pretend we're being attacked
            by poison gas . . . and that.

There's this playground with lines for rounders,
And cricket stumps chalked on the wall,
And kids with their coats for goalposts
Booting a tennis ball
Around all over the place and shoutin' and arguin'
    about offside and they always kick it over
        the garden wall next door and she
            goes potty and tells our head teacher
              and he gets right ratty with
                everybody and stops us playin'
                  football . . .
                    . . . and everything.

We have this rule at our school
You've to wait till the whistle blows
And you can't go in till you hear it
Not even if it snows
And your wellies get filled with water and your socks
    go all soggy and start slipping down your legs
        and your hands get so cold they go all
            crumpled and you can't undo
              the buttons of your mac when
                you do get inside . . .
                . . . it's true.

The best thing is our classroom.
When it's fine you can see right far,
Past the Catholic Cathedral
Right to the Morris Car
Works where me Dad works as a fitter and sets off
   right early every morning in these overalls
      with his snap in this sandwich box and
         a flask of tea and always moanin'
           about the money . . . honest.

In Hall we pray for brotherly love
And sing hymns that are ever so long
And the Head shouts at Linda Nutter
Who's always doing wrong.
She can't keep out of trouble because
   she's always talkin'
      she can't stop our teacher says she
        must have been injected with
         a gramophone needle she talks
        so much and
that made me laugh once
not any more though I've heard it
   too often . . . teachers!

Loving your enemy sounds all right
Until you open your eyes
And you're standing next to Nolan
Who's always telling lies
About me and getting me into trouble and about
   three times a week I fight him after school
      it's like a habit I've got
        but I can't love him even though
         I screw my eyes up real hard and try like
          mad, but if it wasn't him it
           would be somebody else

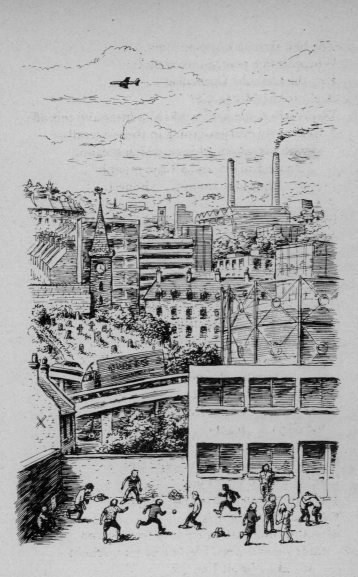

I mean
you've got to have enemies . . .
. . . haven't you?

We sing 'O to be a pilgrim'
And think about God and heaven
And then we're told the football team lost
By thirteen goals to seven
But that's not bad because St Xavier's don't half have
   big lads in their team and last time we played
      they beat us eighteen one and this time
         we got seven goals . . .
           . . . didn't we?

Then we have our lessons,
We have Science and English and Maths,
Except on Wednesday morning
When our class goes to the baths
And it's not half cold and Peter Bradberry's
   fingers went all wrinkled and blue last week
      and I said, 'You're goin' to die, man'
         but he pushed me under the water and I had to
         hold my breath for fifteen minutes.
           But he's still alive though . . .
              . . . he is.

Friday's my favourite day though,
We have Art all afternoon
And I never care what happens
'Cos I know it's home-time soon
And I'm free for two whole days but I think
   sometimes it wouldn't be half so good
      having this weekend if we didn't have five
        days
          of
             school
               in
                 between –
Would it?

Gareth Owen

The ABC

'Twas midnight in the schoolroom
And every desk was shut,
When suddenly from the alphabet
Was heard a loud 'Tut-tut!'

Said A to B, 'I don't like C;
His manners are a lack.
For all I ever see of C
Is a semi-circular back!'

'I disagree,' said D to B,
'I've never found C so.
From where I stand, he seems to be
An uncompleted O.'

C was vexed, 'I'm much perplexed,
You criticize my shape.
I'm made like that, to help spell Cat
And Cow and Cool and Cape.'

'He's right,' said E; said F, 'Whoopee!'
Said G, ''Ip, 'ip, 'ooray!'
'You're dropping me,' roared H to G.
'Don't do it please I pray!'

'Out of my way,' LL said to K.
'I'll make poor I look ILL.'
To stop this stunt, J stood in front,
And presto! ILL was JILL.

'U know,' said V, 'that W
Is twice the age of me,
For as a Roman V is five
I'm half as young as he.'

X and Y yawned sleepily,
'Look at the time!' they said.
'Let's all get off to beddy byes.'
They did, then, 'Z-z-z.'

or, alternative last verse

X and Y yawned sleepily,
Look at the time!' they said.
They all jumped in to beddy byes
And the last one in was Z!

Spike Milligan

Playing Truant

Davy
was no fan
of the School Attendance man

Maybe
canes and schools
aren't really suitable for fools

the Law
still demanded
that school should be attended

what's more
the Headmaster
proclaimed him a disaster

being no
great bookworm
his liking for lessons was lukewarm

even so
he was fluent
in the art of playing truant

Raymond Wilson

Timothy Winters

Timothy Winters comes to school
With eyes as wide as a football-pool,
Ears like bombs and teeth like splinters:
A blitz of a boy is Timothy Winters.

His belly is white, his neck is dark,
And his hair is an exclamation mark.
His clothes are enough to scare a crow
And through his britches the blue winds blow.

When teacher talks he won't hear a word
And he shoots down dead the arithmetic-bird,
He licks the patterns off his plate
And he's not even heard of the Welfare State.

Timothy Winters has bloody feet
And he lives in a house on Suez Street,
He sleeps in a sack on the kitchen floor
And they say there aren't boys like him any more.

Old man Winters likes his beer
And his missus ran off with a bombardier,
Grandma sits in the grate with a gin
And Timothy's dosed with an aspirin.

The Welfare Worker lies awake
But the law's as tricky as a ten-foot snake,
So Timothy Winters drinks his cup
And slowly goes on growing up.

At Morning Prayers the Headmaster helves
For children less fortunate than ourselves,
And the loudest response in the room is when
Timothy Winters roars 'Amen!'

So come one angel, come on ten:
Timothy Winters says 'Amen'
Amen amen amen amen.
Timothy Winters, Lord.

> Amen.

> *Charles Causley*

Percival Mandeville

from *Summoned by Bells*

Percival Mandeville, the perfect boy,
Was all a schoolmaster could wish to see –
Upright and honourable, good at games,
Well-built, blue-eyed; a sense of leadership
Lifted him head and shoulders from the crowd.
His work was good. His written answers, made
In a round, tidy and decided hand,
Pleased the examiners. His open smile
Enchanted others. He could also frown
On anything unsporting, mean or base,
Unworthy of the spirit of the school
And what it stood for. Oh the dreadful hour
When once upon a time he frowned on me!

Just what had happened I cannot recall –
Maybe some bullying in the dormitory;
But well I recollect his warning words:
'I'll fight you, Betjeman, you swine, for that,
Behind the bike shed before morning school.'
So all the previous night I spewed with fear.
I could not box: I greatly dreaded pain.
A recollection of the winding punch
Jack Drayton once delivered, blows and boots
Upon the bum at Highgate Junior School,
All multiplied by X from Mandeville,
Emptied my bladder. Silent in the dorm
I cleaned my teeth and clambered into bed.
Thin seemed pyjamas and inadequate
The regulation blankets once so warm.
'What's up?' 'Oh, nothing.' I expect they knew . . .

And, in the morning, cornflakes, bread and tea,
Cook's Farm Eggs and a spoon of marmalade,
Which heralded the North and Hillard hours
Of Latin composition, brought the post.
Breakfast and letters! Then it was a flash
Of hope, escape and inspiration came:
Invent a letter of bad news from home.
I hung my head and tried to look as though,
By keeping such a brave stiff upper lip
And just not blubbing, I was noble too.
I sought out Mandeville. 'I say,' I said,
'I'm frightfully sorry I can't fight today.
I've just received some rotten news from home:
My mater's very ill.' No need for more –
His arm was round my shoulder comforting:
'All right, old chap. Of course I understand.'

John Betjeman

Sally

She was a dog-rose kind of girl:
elusive, scattery as petals;
scratchy sometimes, tripping you like briars.
She teased the boys
turning this way and that, not to be tamed
or taught any more than the wind.
Even in school the word 'ought'
had no meaning for Sally.
On dull days
she'd sit quiet as a mole at her desk
delving in thought.
But when the sun called
she was gone, running the blue day down
till the warm hedgerows prickled the dusk
and moths flickered out.

Her mother scolded; Dad
gave her the hazel-switch,
said her head was stuffed with feathers
and a starling tongue.
But they couldn't take the shine out of her.
Even when it rained
you felt the sun saved under her skin.
She'd a way of escape
laughing at you from the bright end of a tunnel,
leaving you in the dark.

Phoebe Hesketh

Odd-Job Boy

An odd-job boy, with a face like a boot repair,
His regulation grey school shirts are never crisp
And a right-angled tear is mended in his blazer.
He tightens nuts and bolts and puts screws back
In the glossy modern desks that are shaking to pieces
Or takes the hacksaw to the desklid padlock
Of a boy who has lost his keys. Observant
But uninterested in the academic life,
He passes aslant the school curriculum
On the way to a garage or fitting shop.

Stanley Cook

Johnny Little

Johnny Little was so small
Teacher never saw him.
Climbed on his desk to make himself tall
And tried to stick his oar in.

Teacher, meaning to be kind,
Said, 'Ah, you must be new!
Stay out of trouble. And would you mind
Standing when I speak to you?'

Raymond Wilson

Friends

When first I went to school
I walked with Sally.
She carried my lunch pack,
Told me about a book she'd read
With a handsome hero
So I said,
'You be my best friend.'
After break I went right off her.
I can't say why
And anyway I met Joan
Who's pretty with dark curls
And we sat in a corner of the playground
And giggled about the boy who brought the milk.
Joan upset me at lunch,
I can't remember what she said actually,
But I was definitely upset
And took up with Hilary
Who's frightfully brilliant and everything
And showed me her history
Which I considered very decent.
The trouble with Hilary is
She has to let you know how clever she is
And I said,
'You're not the only one who's clever you know,'
And she went all quiet and funny
And hasn't spoken to me since.
Good riddance I say
And anyway Linda is much more my type of girl;
She does my hair in plaits
And says how pretty I look,
She really says what she thinks
And I appreciate that.

Nadine said she was common
When we saw her on the bus that time
Sitting with three boys from that other school,
And I had to agree
There was something in what she said.
There's a difference between friendliness
And being cheap
And I thought it my duty
To tell her what I thought.
Well she laughed right in my face
And then pretended I wasn't there
So I went right off her.
If there's one thing I can't stand
It's being ignored and laughed at.
Nadine understood what I meant,
Understood right away
And that's jolly nice in a friend.
I must tell you one thing about her,
She's rather a snob.
I get the feeling
She looks down on me
And she'll never come to my house
Though I've asked her thousands of times.
I thought it best to have it out with her
And she went off in a huff
Which rather proved my point
And I considered myself well rid.

At the moment
I walk home on my own
But I'm keeping my eyes open
And when I see somebody I consider suitable
I'll befriend her.

Gareth Owen

I was Mucking About in Class

I was mucking about in class

Mr Brown said,
Get out and take your chair with me
I suppose he *meant* to say
Take your chair with you
so Dave said,
Yeah – you heard what he said
          get out and take my chair with him
so Ken said,
Yeah – get out and take his chair with me
so I said to Mr Brown
Yessir – shall I take our chair with you, sir?

Wow
That meant BIG TROUBLE

Michael Rosen

The Dunce

Why does he still keep ticking?
    Why does his round white face
Stare at me over the books and ink,
    And mock at my disgrace?

Why does that thrush call, 'Dunce, dunce, dunce!'?
    Why does that bluebottle buzz?
Why does the sun so silent shine? –
    And what do I care if he does?

Walter de la Mare

In One Ear and Out the Other

When Miss Tibbs talks
To my dear brother,
It goes in one ear
And out the other.
And when she shouts,
He seldom hears,
The words just whistle
Through his ears.

His ears are big
(You must've seen them),
But he's got nothing
In between them.
The truth, Miss Tibbs,
Is hard to face.
His head is full
Of empty space.

Colin West

Dunce?

Cannot read, cannot spell,
But can swim a length, ride my bike faster than anyone,
go to school on my own and back, use the telephone,
make little buns, do the shopping, crow like a cockerel.

Cannot sing, cannot do sums,
But can milk a cow, feed the chickens, ride a pony, clean
out the pigs, know where first mushrooms grow, look
after my canary, remember to shut gates, catch millers'
thumbs.

And when I can read, spell, do sums and sing,
Shall I then be able to do anything?

Leonard Clark

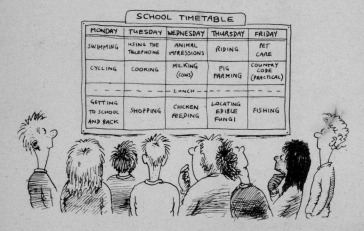

| SCHOOL TIMETABLE | | | | |
MONDAY	TUESDAY	WEDNESDAY	THURSDAY	FRIDAY
SWIMMING	USING THE TELEPHONE	ANIMAL IMPRESSIONS	RIDING	PET CARE
CYCLING	COOKING	MILKING (COWS)	PIG FARMING	COUNTRY CODE (PRACTICAL)
— — — —	— — —	— LUNCH —	— — — —	— — —
GETTING TO SCHOOL AND BACK	SHOPPING	CHICKEN FEEDING	LOCATING EDIBLE FUNGI	FISHING

The Dunce

He says no with his head
but he says yes with his heart
he says yes to what he loves
he says no to the teacher
he stands
he is questioned
and all the problems are posed
sudden laughter seizes him
and he erases all
the words and figures
names and dates
sentences and snares
and despite the teacher's threats
to the jeers of infant prodigies
with chalk of every colour
on the blackboard of misfortune
he draws the face of happiness.

Jacques Prévert
translated from the French by
Lawrence Ferlinghetti

A Boy Left Over

A little nose like an inverted comma
And mousy hair of course, a boy left over
From an elder brother who captained the First Eleven
And the School. Looking abstract and remote
In a saintly way but really rather deaf,
He passes by the mischief of other boys
Like an accident; he blinks at a rebuke.
No pin-ups inside his desk but books as neat
As biscuits in a packet. Ought I to wish
For his own sake that he was sometimes insolent?

Stanley Cook

Nooligan

I'm a nooligan
dont give a toss
in our class
I'm the boss
(well, one of them)

I'm a nooligan
got a nard 'ead
step out of line
and youre dead
(well, bleedin)

I'm a nooligan
I spray me name
all over town
footballs me game
(well, watchin)

I'm a nooligan
violence is fun
gonna be a nassassin
or a nired gun
(well, a soldier)

Roger McGough

Streemin

Im in the botom streme
Which meens Im not brigth
dont like reading
cant hardly write

but all these divishns
arnt reely fair
look at the cemtery
no streemin there

Roger McGough

King of the Toilets

Maurice was King of the Toilets,
The ones by the wall – by the shed,
He ruled with the power and conviction
of a king with a crown on his head.

He entered them FIRST every morning
and he'd sit on the wall by the gate
and wait for the grumpy schoolkeeper
to unlock them – at twenty past eight.

Then he'd rush in with great shouts of triumph
And he'd slam all the doors one by one
And he'd climb on the caretaker's cupboards
And he'd pull all the chains just for fun.

He'd swing on the pipes by the cistern,
And he'd leap from the top of the doors,
And he'd frighten the new little infants –
with bellows and yellings and roars.

He always ate lunch in the toilets,
And he'd sit with his food on the floor,
And check who was coming (or going) –
and kick at the catch on their door.

He once burst the pipe by the outflow,
By climbing right up the tank,
And flooded the lower school library,
With water that gushed out and stank.

He once jammed the door on the end one
with five juniors stuck fast inside,
And bombed them with piles of old comics
Whilst they struggled and shouted and cried.

He was useless in class – and at lessons.
He couldn't do hardly a thing –
But when he was out in the toilets –
THEN MAURICE THE USELESS
WAS KING!

Peter Dixon

The Bully Asleep

This afternoon, when grassy
Scents through the classroom crept,
Bill Craddock laid his head
Down on his desk, and slept.

The children came round him:
Jimmy, Roger, and Jane;
they lifted his head timidly
And let it sink again.

'Look, he's gone sound asleep, Miss,'
Said Jimmy Adair;
'He stays up all the night, you see;
His mother doesn't care.'

'Stand away from him, children.'
Miss Andrews stooped to see.
'Yes, he's asleep; go on
With your writing, and let him be.'

'Now's a good chance!' whispered Jimmy;
And he snatched Bill's pen and hid it.
'Kick him under the desk, hard;
He won't know who did it.'

'Fill all his pockets with rubbish –
Paper, apple-cores, chalk.'
So they plotted, while Jane
Sat wide-eyed at their talk.

Not caring, not hearing,
Bill Craddock he slept on;
Lips parted, eyes closed –
Their cruelty gone.

'Stick him with pins!' muttered Roger.
'Ink down his neck!' said Jim.
But Jane, tearful and foolish,
Wanted to comfort him.

John Walsh

Prep.

One looks absorbed, his eyes detached from all within the
   room;
     Another flashes glances to and fro;
Another yawns, looks idly at a youth in front, to whom
     He presently applies a furtive toe.

Some frankly drowse; some seek their inspiration from the
   wall;
     At fast-decreasing pens their molars chew.
The lounging limbs, the dull, bored eyes are common to
   them all;
     And Heaven only knows what prep. they do.

G. D. Martineau

The Bookworm

'I'm tired – oh, tired of books,' said Jack,
   'I long for meadows green,
And woods where shadowy violets
   Nod their cool leaves between;
I long to see the ploughman stride
   His darkening acres o'er,
To hear the hoarse sea-waters drive
   Their billows 'gainst the shore;
I long to watch the sea-mew wheel
   Back to her rock-perched mate;
Or, where the breathing cows are housed,
   Lean, dreaming, at the gate.
Something has gone, and ink and print
   Will never bring it back;
I long for the green fields again,
   I'm tired of books,' said Jack.

Walter de la Mare

Schoolpoem 2

One day i went into the school library and
           there were no books. Panic-stricken
i looked for explanations in the eyes
           of a school-tied librarian but
she just stamped a date on my wrist
           and said i was overdue.
Then i spied one little book called
           'HOW TO SPELL'
                   but
i new how to do that already,
so i sat feeling pretty lonely
as you can imagine in a bookless library,
           in the skeleton of a library,
going over all the names of books i once new:
           WAR AND PEACE
           DANNY THE DORMOUSE
how nice and neat and safe they were.
Now all i do is look for answers
           in my blazer pockets but
they have gone through the holes
           made by yesterday's
                   marbles.

                        Brian McCabe

Arithmetic

I'm 11. And I don't really know
my Two Times Table. Teacher says it's
    disgraceful
But even if I had the time, I feel too tired.
Ron's 5, Samantha's 3, Carole's 18 months,
and then there's Baby. I do what's required.

Mum's working. Dad's away. And so
I dress them, give them breakfast. Mrs Russell
moves in, and I take Ron to school.
Miss Eames calls me an old-fashioned word:
    Dunce.
Doreen Maloney says I'm a fool.

After tea, to the Rec. Pram-pushing's slow
but on fine days it's a good place, full
of larky boys. When 6 shows on the clock
I put the kids to bed. I'm free for once.
At about 7 – Mum's key in the lock.

Gavin Ewart

Growing Pain

The boy was barely five years old.
We sent him to the little school
And left him there to learn the names
Of flowers in jam jars on the sill.

And learn to do as he was told.
He seemed quite happy there until
Three weeks afterwards, at night,
The darkness whimpered in his room.
I went upstairs, switched on his light
And found him wide awake, distraught,
Sheets mangled and his eiderdown
Untidy carpet on the floor.
I said, 'Why can't you sleep? A pain?'
He snuffled, gave a little moan,
And then he spoke a single word:
'Jessica'. The sound was blurred.
'Jessica? What do you mean?'
'A girl at school called Jessica,
She hurts –' he touched himself between
The heart and stomach '– she has been
Aching here and I can see her.'
Nothing I had read or heard
Instructed me in what to do.
I covered him and stroked his head.
'The pain will go, in time,' I said.

Vernon Scannell

The Pain

Coming home from school when I was seven
I told my mother of the pain.
'Where is the pain?' she asked.
'Here,' I said, holding before me
Two imaginary pillows in the air.

'Where were you when it started?'
'At Farnborough Road Juniors
But then I took it on the bus with me.'
'At what time did the pain start?'
'Between the end of dinner time
And the ringing of the bell for afternoon.'
'Was it something you ate? How did you notice it?'
'It walked through the door of Miss Mellor's classroom.
Before there was just me
After there were two of us, the pain and me.'
'Was anything said, did anybody notice?'
'Something was said about the register,
When the room was empty the pain had made its home
    there.'
'Can't you tell me more?' my mother said,
She was getting bored with this conversation,
'What would you call the pain?'
'The pain is called Nancy Muriel Oliver
And is pale with yellow hair.
Is there nothing you can do, nothing you can say?'
'No,' said my mother, closing the medicine cabinet.
'Just go back to school tomorrow
And pray it never goes away.'

Gareth Owen

Dumb Insolence

I'm big for ten years old
Maybe that's why they get at me

Teachers, parents, cops
Always getting at me

When they get at me

I don't hit em
They can do you for that

I don't swear at em
They can do you for that

I stick my hands in my pockets
And stare at them

And while I stare at them
I think about sick

They call it dumb insolence

They don't like it
But they can't do you for it

I've been done before
They say if I get done again

They'll put me in a home
So I do dumb insolence

Adrian Mitchell

from *The Ranks of Life*

For the Amusement & Instruction of Youth (1821)

A lad when at school one day stole a pin,
And said that no harm was in such a small sin.
He next stole a knife and said 'twas a trifle:
Next thing he did was pockets to rifle.
Next thing he did was a house to break in.
The next thing – upon the gallows to swing.
So let us avoid all little sinnings,
Since such is the end of petty beginnings.

Unknown

A Portrait

I look as if I'm working hard.
At least I *hope* I do:
I have to keep one eye on guard,
Since Art, in Prep., is strictly barred,
And, if old Marty knew
That I had sketched his features in
With such a perfect touch,
Displaying where his hair grows thin,
I say – if he observed my sin,
I wouldn't like it much.

It's not that I can really draw,
Or that I want to try;
In fact I hardly care a straw
For Art that does not break the law
Beneath a master's eye.
Each time his glance comes roving round
I grow intent and brisk.
I scowl and give a worried sound . . .
One likes to think it *might* be found;
The thought is worth the risk!

G. D. Martineau

Homework Machine

The Homework Machine, oh the Homework Machine,
Most perfect contraption that's ever been seen.
Just put in your homework, then drop in a dime,
Snap on the switch, and in ten seconds' time,
Your homework comes out, quick and clean as can be.
Here it is – 'nine plus four?' and the answer is 'three.'
Three?
Oh me . . .
I guess it's not as perfect
As I thought it would be.

Shel Silverstein

Blackboard Jungle

'Smith is dead, sir, killed yesterday after school. Did you
    know?'
My pupils jostled round me, all agog to tell me so.
Obviously they found this sudden end of one they knew,
    thrilling:
Life for a while was different in this killing.
How Smith died, what the car did to him and his bike,
Was the talk of the school that morning, the like
Of nothing on the telly or in sport;
Smith, for once and for all time, had caught
The imaginations of his fellows, who never saw
Much to talk about in him before.
His form-mates wondered if he hadn't really come off
    best:
'Just like Smith to go and miss the Latin test.'

By dinner-time he was forgotten. Boys
At their allotted task with food no longer heard the voice
Of one crying in the wilderness of death.
They saved their breath
To cool their pudding.
      Three days later Smith was burnt.

I tell the tale, am not sure of the moral to be learnt:
Cruelty, thy name is childhood; ignorance is bliss –
Something of the sort perhaps.

      I add by way of postscript this:
Overheard: 'I say, have you heard the latest joke?
About how black Smith looked when he went up in
    smoke?'

Julian Ennis

The Lesson

'Your father's gone,' my bald headmaster said.
His shiny dome and brown tobacco jar
Splintered at once in tears. It wasn't grief.
I cried for knowledge which was bitterer
Than any grief. For there and then I knew
That grief has uses – that a father dead
Could bind the bully's fist a week or two;
And then I cried for shame, then for relief.

I was a month past ten when I learnt this:
I still remember how the noise was stilled
In school-assembly when my grief came in.
Some goldfish in a bowl quietly sculled
Around their shining prison on its shelf.
They were indifferent. All the other eyes
Were turned towards me. Somewhere in myself
Pride, like a goldfish, flashed a sudden fin.

Edward Lucie-Smith

Mid-Term Break

I sat all morning in the college sick bay
Counting bells knelling classes to a close.
At two o'clock our neighbours drove me home.

In the porch I met my father crying –
he had always taken funerals in his stride –
And Big Jim Evans saying it was a hard blow.

The baby cooed and laughed and rocked the pram
When I came in, and I was embarrassed
By old men standing up to shake my hand

And tell me they were 'sorry for my trouble',
Whispers informed strangers I was the eldest,
Away at school, as my mother held my hand

In hers and coughed out angry tearless sighs.
At ten o'clock the ambulance arrived
With the corpse, stanched and bandaged by the nurses.

Next morning I went up into the room. Snowdrops
And candles soothed the bedside; I saw him
For the first time in six weeks. Paler now,

Wearing a poppy bruise on his left temple,
He lay in the four foot box as in his cot.
No gaudy scars, the bumper knocked him clear.

A four foot box, a foot for every year.

Seamus Heaney

Romance

When I was but thirteen or so
   I went into a golden land,
Chimborazo, Cotopaxi
   Took me by the hand.

My father died, my brother too,
   They passed like fleeting dreams,
I stood where Popocatapetl
   In the sunlight gleams.

I dimly heard the master's voice
   And boys far off at play,
Chimborazo, Cotopaxi
   Had stolen me away.

I walked in a great golden dream
  To and fro from school –
Shining Popocatapetl
  The dusty streets did rule.

I walked home with a gold dark boy
  And never a word I'd say,
Chimborazo, Cotopaxi
  Had taken my speech away:

I gazed entranced upon his face
  Fairer than any flower –
O shining Popocatapetl
  It was thy magic hour:

The houses, people, traffic seemed
  Thin fading dreams by day,
Chimborazo, Cotopaxi
  Had stolen my soul away!

                    W. J. Turner

An Injection

We stampede down the corridor,
Each holding a white card,
Fingering it like some poisonous insect.
Will it hurt?
The thud of our feet echoes our drumming hearts.
'Bags last!'
'I'm going last.'
'I'm not going first.'
'Me neither.'
We stand in line,
Like prisoners waiting for execution.
I'm not scared.
I try to sound heroic.
I drift . . .
Into a senseless dream.
I snap out of it as my friend jolts me.
Saying, 'Go on, it's you next.'
I march stiffly towards the door.
The nurse motions me to the chair.
The saliva refuses to enter my mouth.
The blue-flamed bunsen-burner hisses slightly.
The drab, grey walls seem more depressing than usual.
My sleeve is pushed roughly up.
The strong stench of disinfectant bites my nostrils.
My arm is touched with something cold.
I shudder violently.
It brushes my arm
Soothingly.
Everyone falls silent.
It's over!
A mere pin prick.

A bubble of blood
Dribbles down my arm.
It's absorbed by a piece of lint.
A gush of breath rushes out.
The air seems clearer.
My mind fresher.
'Next please.'

Janet Clark
aged 12

School Dinners

If you stay to school dinners
Better throw them aside;
A lot of kids didn't,
A lot of kids died.

The meat is made of iron,
The spuds are made of steel;
And if that don't get you
the afters will!

Unknown

Tomato Sauce

If you do not shake the bottle.
None'll come, and then a lot'll.

Unknown

Skipping Song

Anne and Belinda
Turning the rope
Helen jumps in
But she hasn't got a hope.
Helen Freckles
What will you do?
Skip on the table
In the Irish stew.
Freckles on her face
Freckles on her nose
Freckles on her bum
Freckles on her toes.

Helen Freckles
Tell me true
How many freckles
Have you got on you?
One-two-three-four-five-six-seven
And out goes you.

Stella Starwars
Skip in soon
Into your space-ship
And off to the moon.
Skip on the pavement
One and two
Skip like a rabbit
Or a kangaroo.
Skip so high
You never come down
Over the steeples
Over the town.
Skip over rooftops
Skip over trees
Skip over rivers
Skip over seas.
Skip over London
Skip over Rome
Skip all night
And never come home.
Skip over moonbeams
Skip over Mars
Skip through the Milky Way
And try to count the stars.
One-two-three-four-five-six-seven
Out goes you.

Gareth Owen

In the Playground

In the playground
Some run round
Chasing a ball
Or chasing each other;
Some pretend to be
Someone on TV;
Some walk
And talk,
Some stand
On their hands
Against the wall
And some do nothing at all.

Stanley Cook

The Playground

from 'A Peep into a Poor-Law School'

Nor was hopscotch disdained by some,
Played with their sisters when at home;
And tops, and hoops, and marbles came,
As seasons changed their every game,
The same old round as now we see,
Which surely is a mystery;
No cricket bat did any wield,
For there was then no playing-field,
For 'rounders' there was room enough,
No football, though some games as rough;
And they rejoiced in flying kites,
The smaller boys with little mites,
Made from the leaves of copy-books,
The outcome oft of saddened looks . . .

James Harvey

Winter

On Winter mornings in the playground
The boys stand huddled,
Their cold hands doubled
Into trouser pockets.
The air hangs frozen
About the buildings
And the cold is an ache in the blood
And a pain on the tender skin
Beneath finger nails.
The odd shouts
Sound off like struck iron
And the sun
Balances white
Above the boundary wall.
I fumble my bus ticket
Between numb fingers
Into a fag,
Take a drag
And blow white smoke
Into the December air.

Gareth Owen

The Playground

Be it a weakness, it deserves some praise,
We love the play-place of our early days;
The scene is touching, and the heart is stone
That feels not at that sight, and feels at none.
The wall on which we tried our graving skill,
The very name we carved subsisting still;
The bench on which we sat while deep employed,
Though mangled, hacked, and hewed, not yet destroyed;
The little ones, unbuttoned, glowing hot,
Playing our games, and on the very spot;
As happy as we once, to kneel and draw
The chalky ring, and knuckle down at taw;
To pitch the ball into the grounded hat,
Or drive it devious with a dexterous pat;
The pleasing spectacle at once excites
Such collection of our own delights,
That, viewing it, we seem almost to obtain
Our innocent, sweet, simple years again.

William Cowper

Dog in the Playground

Dog in the playground
Suddenly there.
Smile on his face,
Tail in the air.

Dog in the playground
Bit of a fuss:
I know that dog –
Lives next to us!

Dog in the playground:
Oh, no he don't.
He'll come with me,
You see if he won't.

The word gets round;
The crowd gets bigger.
His name's Bob.
It ain't – it's Trigger.

They call him Archie!
They call him Frank!
Lives by the Fish Shop!
Lives up the Bank!
Who told you that?
Pipe down! Shut up!
I know that dog
Since he was a pup.

Dog in the playground:
We'll catch him, Miss.
Leave it to us.
Just watch this!

Dog in the playground
What a to-do!
Thirty-five children,
Caretaker too,
Chasing the dog,
Chasing each other.
I know that dog –
He's our dog's brother!

We've cornered him now;
He can't get away.
Told you we'd catch him,
Robert and   Hey!
Don't open that door –
Oh, Glenis, you fool!
Look, Miss, what's happened:
Dog in the school.

Dog in the classroom,
Dog in the hall,
Dog in the toilets –
He's paying a call!
Forty-six children,
Caretaker too,
Headmaster, three teachers,
Hullabaloo!

Lost him! Can't find him!
He's vanished! And then:
Look, Miss, he's back
In the playground again.

Shouting and shoving
I'll give you what for!
Sixty-five children
Head for the door.

Dog in the playground,
Smile on his face,
Tail in the air,
Winning the race.

Dog in his element
Off at a jog,
Out of the gates:
Wish I was a dog.

Dog in the playground:
Couldn't he run?

Dog in the playground
    . . . Gone!

Allan Ahlberg

He Who Owns the Whistle
Rules the World

january wind and the sun
playing truant again.
Rain beginning to scratch
its fingernails across
the blackboard sky

in the playground
kids divebomb, corner
at silverstone or execute
traitors. Armed
with my Acme Thunderer
I step outside,
take a deep breath
and bring the world
to a standstill

Roger McGough

Playground Game

As I went down the school yard
  Down among the bullies, O,
They shouted at me good and hard
  Kiss a girl and let her go.

And there were Mary, Ruth and Jean
  Down among the bullies, O,
The prettiest girls you've ever seen
  Kiss a girl and let her go.

Jean, Ruth and Mary gave a look so quick
  Down among the bullies, O,
To see which one of them I'd pick
  Kiss a girl and let her go.

The crowd stood round me like a wall
  Down among the bullies, O,
I ran and dodged them one and all
  Kiss a girl and let her go.

They cornered me by the cycle shed
  Down among the bullies, O,
'Pick one of them or we'll punch your head!'
  Kiss a girl and let her go.

I chose Kathy Brown with the mousy hair
  Down among the bullies, O,
Who hadn't a boy and didn't care
  Kiss a girl and let her go.

She thought she was ugly, Kathy Brown,
   Down among the bullies, O,
Everyone thought I was playing the clown
   Kiss a girl and let her go.

Our dry lips met for less than a second
   Down among the bullies, O,
The damage done will never be reckoned
   Kiss a girl and let her go.

Her eyes came alight as they'd never been
   Down among the bullies, O,
Their shadow fell on Mary, Ruth and Jean
   And the girl I kissed I'll never let go.

                    Raymond Wilson

The Loner

He leans against the playground wall,
Smacks his hands against the bricks
And other boredom-beating tricks,
Traces patterns with his feet,
Scuffs to make the tarmac squeak,
Back against the wall he stays –
And never plays.

The playground's quick with life,
The beat is strong.
Though sharp as a knife
Strife doesn't last long.
There is shouting, laughter, song,
And a place at the wall
For who won't belong.

We pass him running, skipping, walking,
In slow huddled groups, low talking.
Each in our familiar clique
We pass him by and never speak,
His loneness is his shell and shield
And neither he nor we will yield.

He wasn't there at the wall today,
Someone said he'd moved away
To another school and place
And on the wall where he used to lean
Someone had chalked
'watch this space'.

Julie Holder

from *New Boy's View of Rugger*

When first I played I nearly died.
   The bitter memory still rankles –
They formed a scrum with *me* inside!
   Some kicked the ball and some my ankles.
I did not like the game at all,
   Yet, after all the harm they'd done me,
Whenever I came near the ball
   They knocked me down and stood upon me.

Rupert Brooke
from a school magazine of 1904

I Ran for a Catch

I ran for a catch
   With the sun in my eyes, sir,
Being sure of a 'snatch'
   I ran for a catch . . .
Now I wear a black patch
   And a nose *such* a size, sir,
I ran for a catch
   With the sun in my eyes, sir.

Coulson Kernahan

Conkers

When chestnuts are hanging
Above the school yard,
They are little green sea-mines
Spiky and hard.

But when they fall bursting
And all the boys race,
Each shines like a jewel
In a satin case.

Clive Sansom

The School Field in December

Hundreds of Wellington boots
have trampled the snow until
the field glitters like a rink.

Snowmen stand rigid with cold.
Squeals of children skate across
this acre of Arctic ice.

Wes Magee

Lock Up Your Javelins

When I checked the gymnasium store
    There were only three javelins there:
I knew that there ought to be four
When I checked the gymnasium store,
But I couldn't discover one more
    Though I searched for a long time with care:
When I checked the gymnasium store
    There were only three javelins there.

I knew I should speak to the Head –
    So I knocked, and walked in at his door;
I ought to have waited instead,
But an urgent thing had to be said:
So I barged in, and – there he was – dead!
    By a javelin pinned to the floor!
I did want to speak to the Head,
    But now he won't talk any more.

Kenneth Kitchin

Olympic Special

'It's Olympic Special!'

'And now over to David Coleman
for the start
of the 4 × 100 metres relay heats.'

'Welcome back to the Athletics Stadium
for the 4 × 100 metres relay.
The British Team are in Lane One
and first to run is Hauck . . .'

Hauck. Mick Hauck.
He punched me in the corridor.
I mean he punched me in the belly
in the corridor.
I got him in a headlock
over the knee
on the ground
knee on the chest
and then –
well . . . then to the head's office.

While we were waiting outside the office
he said, 'Look, Rosie,
the head'll say, "What do you think you were doing?"
then he'll say, "Why?" – He always says, "Why?"
Say, you don't know. You were being stupid.'

We go in
The head says to Mick Hauck
'What do you think you were doing?'
'I don't know, sir,' Mick Hauck says.

He turns to me.
'Why were you fighting?' he says.
'I was being stupid, sir,' I say.
'You're telling me,' he says.
'Can't you stop being stupid?' he says.
'No, sir,' says Mick Hauck.
'For godssake just try, will you,' he says . . .

'. . . and they're under starter's orders
and they're OFF
Hauck is holding well against Badenski in Lane 2 . . .'

Outside his office
Hauck said, 'I always tell him I was being stupid,
because that's what *he* thinks.
Then he can't think of anything else to say, can he?'

Michael Rosen

A Fight at School

from 'A Boy's Poem'

Upon a day of wind and heavy rain
A crowd was huddling in the porch at school:
As I came up I heard a voice cry out,
'Ho, ho! here comes the lad who talks with ghosts,
Sitting upon the graves.' They laughed and jeered,
And gathered round me in a mocking ring,
And hurt me with their faces and their eyes.
With bitter words I smote them in my hate,
As with a weapon. A sudden blow, and wrath
Sprang upward like a flame. I struck, and blood,
Brighter than rubies, gleamed upon my hand;
And at the beauteous sight, from head to heel
A tiger's joy ran tingling through my veins,
And every finger hungered for a throat.
I burst the broken ring, and darted off
With my blood boiling, and my pulses mad.
I did not feel the rain upon my face;
With burning mouth I drank the cooling wind; –
And then, as if my limbs were touched by death,
A shudder shook me, all the rage that sprang
Like sudden fire in a deserted house
Making the windows fierce, had passed away;
And the cold rain beat heavy on me now;
The winds went through me.

Alexander Smith

A Hot Day at the School

All day long the sun glared
as fiercely as a cross Headteacher.

Out on the brown, parched field
we trained hard for next week's Sports Day.

Hedges wilted in the heat;
teachers' cars sweltered on the tarmac.

In the distance, a grenade of thunder
exploded across the glass sky.

Wes Magee

Build a Bonfire

Build a bonfire, build a bonfire,
Put the teachers on the top;
Put the prefects in the middle,
And we'll burn the blooming lot.

Unknown

The Schoolmaster

Beside yon straggling fence that skirts the way,
With blossomed furze unprofitably gay,
There, in his noisy mansion, skilled to rule,
The village master taught his little school;
A man severe he was, and stern to view,
I knew him well, and every truant knew;
Well had the boding tremblers learned to trace
The day's disasters in his morning face;
Full well they laughed with counterfeited glee
At all his jokes, for many a joke had he;
Full well the busy whisper, circling round,
Conveyed the dismal tidings when he frowned;
Yet he was kind, or, if severe in aught,
The love he bore to learning was in fault;
The village all declared how much he knew;
'Twas certain he could write, and cypher too;
Lands he could measure, terms and tides presage,
And even the story ran that he could gauge;
In arguing too, the parson owned his skill,
For e'en though vanquished, he could argue still;
While words of learnèd length and thundering sound
Amazed the gazing rustics ranged around,
And still they gazed, and still the wonder grew,
That one small head could carry all he knew.

Oliver Goldsmith

Blame

Graham, look at Maureen's leg,
She says you tried to tattoo it!
I did, Miss, yes – with my biro,
But Jonathan told me to do it.

Graham, look at Peter's sock,
It's got a burn-hole through it!
It was just an experiment, Miss, with the lens.
Jonathan told me to do it.

Alice's bag is stuck to the floor,
Look, Graham, did you glue it?
Yes, but I never thought it would work,
And Jonathan told me to do it.

Jonathan, what's all this I hear
About you and Graham Prewitt?
Well, Miss, it's really more his fault:
He *tells* me to tell him to do it.

Allan Ahlberg

Listen While You Speak!

Don't say you are right too often, teacher.
Let the students realize it.
Don't push the truth:
It's not good for it.
Listen while you speak!

Bertolt Brecht
translated from the German

Schoolmaster

The window gives onto the white trees.
The master looks out of it at the trees,
for a long time, he looks for a long time
out through the window at the trees,
breaking his chalk slowly in one hand.
And it's only the rules of long division.
And he's forgotten the rules of long division.
Imagine not remembering long division!
A mistake on the blackboard, a mistake.
We watch him with a different attention
needing no one to hint to us about it,
there's more than difference in this attention.
The schoolmaster's wife has gone away,
we do not know where she has gone to,
we do not know why she has gone,
what we know is his wife has gone away.

His clothes are neither new nor in the fashion;
wearing the suit which he always wears
and which is neither new nor in the fashion
the master goes downstairs to the cloakroom.
He fumbles in his pocket for a ticket.
'What's the matter? Where is that ticket?
Perhaps I never picked up my ticket.
Where is the thing?' Rubbing his forehead.
'Oh, here it is. I'm getting old.
Don't argue, auntie dear, I'm getting old.
You can't do much about getting old.'
We hear the door below creaking behind him.

The window gives onto the white trees.
The trees there are high and wonderful,
but they are not why we are looking out.
We look in silence at the schoolmaster.
He has a bent back and clumsy walk,
he moves without defences, clumsily,
worn out I ought to have said, clumsily.
Snow falling on him softly through silence
turns him to white under the white trees.
He whitens into white like the trees.
A little longer will make him so white
we shall not see him in the whitened trees.

Yevgeny Yevtushenko
translated from the Russian by
Robin Milner-Gulland and Peter Levi

The Crib

He said we used a crib.
It did no good to fib.
He'd all the proof he needed:
He used the same as we did.

Guy Boas

A Sense of Vocation

The vast majority of teachers
Are high-souled idealistic creatures:
They don't care a damn
So long as you pass the Exam.

Kenneth Kitchin

School Inspection

'Well, what do you say?' the Inspector asked.
    'Just speak up! There's no need for thinking.'
'But if I don't think, how can I know
    What to say?' Mary answered him, blinking.

'Just blurt it out, girl! Say what you think,
    Without caring what words you may use.'
'But how can I speak,' said Mary, 'until
    I've decided which words I should choose?'

'Simply say what you mean,' the Inspector groaned,
    'Without all this absurd delay.'
'But how can I *tell* what I mean, Sir,
    Till I've heard what I've had to say!'

Raymond Wilson

Duty of the Student

It is the duty of the student
Without exception to be prudent.
If smarter than his teacher, tact
Demands that he conceal the fact.

Edward Anthony

Miss Buss and Miss Beale

Miss Buss and Miss Beale
Cupid's darts do not feel.
O how different from us
Are Miss Beale and Miss Buss!

Unknown

(Miss Beale and Miss Buss were headmistresses
at Cheltenham Ladies' College.)

A Rolling Stone

A rolling stone with the figure for it,
Rumour had it among the younger boys
That once he rode at a seaside Wall of Death
(He did) and his wife was an ex-stripteaser
(She was). He sometimes yelled for quiet
But couldn't do a thing with discipline;
A few more serious boys drew up to his desk
For snatches of education, underheard,
Below the general din, and once in a while
He held the whole of the class as he reminisced
On subjects useless for examinations
But pleasant as eating an apple in class.

Stanley Cook

Teachers' Features

Recalling my own schooldays I have very often thought
That the features of the teachers were a torture to the
    taught:
In view of which, a question I must seriously ask
Is: Wouldn't it be better if a teacher wore a mask?

Kenneth Kitchin

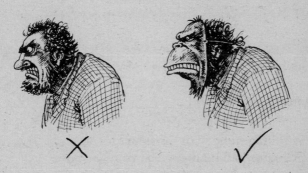

If the Teacher was a Robot

If the teacher was a robot,
Made of Iron and Tin
We could take it all to pieces
And put it in the bin.
We'd loosen all its nuts and bolts
In the metalwork room,
We would weld its mouth tight shut,
And send it to its doom.

Paul Marsh
aged 13

Distracted the Mother Said to Her Boy

Distracted the mother said to her boy,
'Do you try to upset and perplex and annoy?
Now, give me four reasons – and don't play the fool –
Why you shouldn't get up and get ready for school.'

Her son replied slowly, 'Well, mother, you see,
I can't stand the teachers and they detest me;
And there isn't a boy or a girl in the place
That I like or, in turn, that delights in my face.'

'And I'll give you two reasons,' she said, 'why you ought
Get yourself off to school before you get caught;
Because, first, you are forty, and, next, you young fool,
It's your job to be there.
You're the head of the school.'

Gregory Harrison

Rodge Said

Rodge said,
'Teachers – they want it all ways –
You're jumping up and down on a chair
or something
and they grab hold of you and say,
"Would you do that sort of thing in your own home?"

'So you say, "No."
And they say,
"Well don't do it here then."

'But if you say, "Yes, I do it at home,"
they say,
"Well, we don't want that sort of thing
going on here
thank you very much."

'Teachers – they get you all ways,'
Rodge said.

Michael Rosen

The Chemistry Hour

Now let me praise, not famous men,
But men who, for little reward,
Scattered the floor of my dusty pen
With crumbs of truth from a cherished hoard,
And in particular him who came
On Tuesday and Friday, praise the Lord,
Hoping to set our hearts aflame
With natural science, combustible stuff.

Snobs every one of us, lost to shame,
We saw he was shabby and thought him rough.
He wore a beard instead of a tie.
His proud experiments never came off.
And when we applauded, wild with joy,
The splintering glass, the loud explosion,
Anger burned in his ageing eye
But how to quell us he hadn't a notion.
Lost, bewildered, a baited bear,
He'd stand and suffer the loud commotion,
With fluttering hands would stand and swear.

Our regular rioting got him the sack,
Tuesday arrived and he wasn't there:
Some were regretful and felt his lack.
A gentle spirit, fatherly kind,
He always took his punishments back
At the end of class, if only you whined,
Or else forgot them as soon as given,
Having no room in his large mind
For misdemeanours, for sinners unshriven,
For impositions, for 'lines' and such;
He would forgive until seventy times seven.

O rare Mr Robson, I owe you much:
You taught me more than I knew, although,
Of chemistry, nothing remains in my clutch
But the watery marriage of H and O.

Gerald Bullett

Friday

Friday; the clock ticks on to four;
A week of school survived once more;
Teachers smiling, acting friendly,
Feeling, like the kids, weekendly.
Ahead, two days, and all that fun –
Untouched, intact, not yet begun;
Monday's a million miles away,
There's time to please yourself and play.
Nice-as-pie day, clear-blue-sky day:
Why can't all days feel like Friday?

Eric Finney

Friday Morning Last Two Lessons
is Games Day

We straggle in twos
Down Endbutt Lane to the playing fields,
In a gap-toothed murmuring line
Filling the pavement.
Mr Pearson strides out in front
The ball tucked firmly under one arm,
His head bent.

We avoid lampposts
And young mothers pushing prams,
Sometimes walk gammy-legged in gutters
Or scuffle through damp leaves.
The morning is filled
With laughter-tongued and pottering mongrels;
Old men tending bare borders
Slowly unbend
And lean upon their brooms to watch us pass.
Their wives in flowered pinnies
Peer through the lace curtains
Of unused front rooms.

At the pitch
We change in the old pavilion
That smells of dust and feet
And has knot holes in the boarding.
Someone
From another class
Has left
One
Blue and white sock behind.

The lads shout about other games
And goals and saves and shots
Or row about who'll wear red or blue.
Pearson blows exasperation
Briskly through his whistle,
'Come on, lads, let's be having you.'

With eighteen a side
We tear after the ball shouting,
Longing to give it a good clean belt,
Perform some piece of perfection –
Beat three sprawling backs in a mazy dribble,
Race full pelt onto a plate-laid-on pass
And crack it full of hate and zest
Past the diving goalie to bulge the net.
But there is no net
And we have to leg it after the ball
To the allotments by the lane
Before we can take centre
To start the game again.

Afterwards,
Still wearing football socks,
Studded boots slung on my shoulder,
I say 'Tarrah' to Trev
At Station Road and drift home
Playing the game again.
Smoke climbs steep from neat red chimneys;
Babies drool and doze
And laugh at the empty sky.
There is the savour of cabbage and gravy
About the Estate and the flowers do not hear
The great crowd roaring me on.

Gareth Owen

Character Building

Spanking is something that must go,
Say some psychologists, although
Character building is a feat
Sometimes accomplished through the seat.

Edward Anthony

Mr Twackum

Mr Twackum's a very good man,
He goes to church on Sunday.
He prays that God will give him strength
To whack the kids on Monday.

Unknown

The Best of School

The blinds are drawn because of the sun,
And the boys and the room in a colourless gloom
Of underwater float: bright ripples run
Across the walls as the blinds are blown
To let the sunlight in; and I,
As I sit on the shores of the class, alone,
Watch the boys in their summer blouses
As they write, their round heads busily bowed:
And one after another rouses
His face to look at me,
To ponder very quietly,
As seeing, he does not see.

And then he turns again, with a little, glad
Thrill of his work he turns again from me,
Having found what he wanted, having got what was to
    be had.

And very sweet it is, while the sunlight waves
In the ripening morning, to sit alone with the class
And feel the stream of awakening ripple and pass
From me to the boys, whose brightening souls it laves
For this little hour.

                This morning, sweet it is
To feel the lads' looks light on me,
Then back in a swift, bright flutter to work;
Each one darting away with his
Discovery, like birds that steal and flee.

Touch after touch I feel on me
As their eyes glance at me for the grain
Of rigour they taste delightedly.

As tendrils reach out yearningly,
Slowly rotate till they touch the tree
That they cleave unto, and up which they climb
Up to their lives – so they to me.

I feel them cling and cleave to me
As vines going eagerly up; they twine
My life with other leaves, my time
Is hidden in theirs, their thrills are mine.

D. H. Lawrence

School in the Holidays

A week of holiday reconciling me to work
I go up to school for the necessary books
And find the cleaning ladies in their jumble sale buys
Have established depots of buckets and bins
That the boys not there do not kick over
Along the corridor and the caretaker has reeled
Eels of flex out from the power points to the
    floor-polishers.
In my own classroom the portraits I have stood for
In felt-tipped pen and ink have been washed off
The wooden pages of desks towards the back:
Who was the Mary so many boys loved last term
And who wrote 'I hate Sir' and 'I love me'?
'They ought to have detention,' one lady says.
'And clean up the muck they've made,' wishing herself
Out of a job now she has everything
Spick as a sick room. But what are they doing now?

Reading comics in bare feet in front of the fire
And letting their sisters go the errands, I should think.
Covering the carpet with records of pop
Like overlapping lilies on a pond
And behaving in some way or other like little men.

Stanley Cook

Epitaph on a Schoolmaster

Here lie Willie Michie's banes:
    O Satan! when ye tak' him,
Gi'e him the schoolin' o' your weans,
    For clever de'ils he'll mak' 'em!

Robert Burns

(Willie Michie was schoolmaster
of Cleish in Fifeshire.)

Epitaph

A schoolmistress called Binks lies here.
She held her own for twenty year.
She pleaded, biffed, said: 'I'm your friend.'
But children got her in the end.

Roy Fuller

Out of School

Four o'clock strikes,
There's a rising hum,
Then the doors fly open,
The children come.

With a wild cat-call
And a hop-scotch hop
And a bouncing ball
And a whirling top,

Grazing of knees,
A hair pull and a slap,
A hitched-up satchel,
A pulled-down cap,

Bully boys reeling off,
Hurt ones squealing off,
Aviators wheeling off,
Mousy ones stealing off,

Woollen gloves for chilblains,
Cotton rags for snufflers,
Pigtails, coat-tails,
Tails of mufflers,

Machinegun cries,
A kennelful of snarlings,
A hurricane of leaves,
A treeful of starlings,

Thinning away now
By some and some,
Thinning away, away,
All gone home.

Hal Summers

School's Out

Girls scream,
   Boys shout;
Dogs bark,
   School's out.

Cats run
   Horses shy;
Into trees
   Birds fly.

Babes wake
   Open-eyed.
If they can,
   Tramps hide.

Old man,
   Hobble home;
Merry mites,
   Welcome.

W. H. Davies

Evening Schoolboys

Hark to that happy shout! – the school-house door
   Is open thrown, and out the younkers teem;
Some run to leap-frog on the rushy moor,
   And others dabble in the shallow stream,
Catching young fish, and turning pebbles o'er
   For mussel-clams. Look in that mellow gleam,
Where the retiring sun, that rests the while,
   Streams through the broken hedge! How happy seem
Those friendly schoolboys leaning o'er the stile,
   Both reading in one book! – Anon a dream,
Rich with new joys, doth their young hearts beguile,
   And the book's pocketed right hastily.
Ah, happy boys! well may ye turn and smile,
   When joys are yours that never cost a sigh.

John Clare

Holiday

When the boys came out of school they threw up their
    caps,
And the air was striped with their spinning.
When the girls came out of school they pulled off their
    stockings,
And the roof-tops streamed with long black banners.
When the boys and girls came out of school
All the bells of the town choked with their chiming.
When the boys walked in the streets their shoes purred on
    the asphalt,
And the corners were bright as butterflies.
When the girls walked in the streets their legs shone in
    shop-windows,
And the cinema-queues trembled with love.
When the boys and girls walked in the streets
It was like a cathedral decked with worshippers.
And when the boys and girls went back to school
All the clocks of the town wrung their rusted hands.

Julian Mitchell

For a Junior School Poetry Book

The mothers are waiting in the yard.
Here come the children, fresh from school.
The mothers are wearing rumpled skirts.
What prim mouths, what wrinkly cheeks.
The children swirl through the air to them,
trailing satchels and a smell of chalk.

138

The children are waiting in the yard.
The mothers come stumbling out of school.
The children stare primly at them,
lace their shoes, pat their heads.
The mothers swirl through the air to cars.
The children crossly drive them home.

The mothers are coming.
The children are waiting.
The mothers had eyes that see
boiled eggs, wool, dung and bed.
The children have eyes that saw
owl and mountain and little mole.

Christopher Middleton

Bus Home

The school bus now
With seated load
Moves home along
The Beechwood Road.

Blistered of paint,
And old of years,
It takes the rise
With grunt of gears.

Conductor idle,
Slumped and slack;
Driver with square
And jerkin'd back;

And we in cushioned
Seats at ease,
Hushed by the day's
Activities.

All are subdued.
Even young Bill,
Whose tongue is hardly
Ever still,

Seems drowsy as
He quietly chatters
About the most
Unheard-of matters.

Half-sleepy Jim
Kneels on the seat,
Scanning the passers-
by to greet

His friends and foes
With cheerful grins
Or tongue pushed out.
The Glinnis twins

Mingle their hair
Over one book,
Or turn their eyes
With giggling look

To where Bob Morris,
Bat across knee,
Licks his ice-lolly
Thoughtfully.

*

But when we've topped
The Beechwood Rise,
The sudden sun
Strikes in our eyes,

Flooding the bus
With brighter air,
Gleaming on spectacles
And hair.

The old driver jerks
Himself from sleep,
Gripping the wheel
With startled grip,

And in the strong
Light strains and blinks,
Steering his way
By Beechwood Links.

Till now his road,
Swerved from the sun,
Unrolls its shining
Downhill run;

Furrow and field
And farm and oast
Slanting away
To meet the coast.

Fresh comes the off-
shore wind; and we,
Aroused at last
By the smelt sea,

Bestir ourselves
To livelier watch,
Intent our daily
Glimpse to catch

Through Saltings Gap
(A glimpse, no more)
Of the white fringe
On Saltings shore.

A fringe of shore,
A frisk of foam . . .
Then the school bus
Rolls gently home.

John Walsh

Walking from School

from *Summoned by Bells*

Walking from school is a consummate art:
Which routes to follow to avoid the gangs,
Which paths to find that lead, circuitous,
To leafy squirrel haunts and plopping ponds,
For dreams of Archibald and Tiger Tim;
Which hiding-place is safe, and when it is;
What time to leave to dodge the enemy.
I only once was trapped. I knew the trap –
I heard it in their tones: 'Walk back with us.'
I knew they weren't my friends; but that soft voice
Wheedled me from my route to cold Swain's Lane.
There in a holly bush they threw me down,
Pulled off my shorts, and laughed and ran away;
And, as I struggled up, I saw grey brick,
The cemetery railings, and the tombs.

John Betjeman

The Place's Fault

Once, after a rotten day at school –
Sweat on my fingers, pages thumbed with smears,
Cane smashing down to make me keep them neat –
I blinked out to the sunlight and the heat
And stumbled up the hill, still swallowing tears.
A stone hissed past my ear – 'Yah! gurt fat fool!'

Some urchins waited for me by my gate.
I shouted swear-words at them, walked away.
'Yeller,' they yelled, "e's yeller!' And they flung
Clods, stones, bricks – anything to make me run.
I ran, all right, up hill all scorching day
With 'yeller' in my ears. 'I'm not, I'm not!'

Another time, playing too near the shops –
Oddly no doubt, I'm told I was quite odd,
Making, no doubt, a noise – a girl in slacks
Came out and told some kids 'Run round the back,
Bash in his back door, smash up his back yard,
And if he yells I'll go and fetch the cops.'

And what a rush I had to lock those doors
Before that rabble reached them! What desire
I've had these twenty years to lock away
That place where fingers pointed out my play,
Where even the grass was tangled with barbed wire,
Where through the streets I waged continual wars!

We left (it was a temporary halt)
The knots of ragged kids, the wired-off beach,
Faces behind the blinds. I'll not return;
There's nothing there I haven't had to learn,
And I've learned nothing that I'd care to teach –
Except that I know it was the place's fault.

Philip Hobsbaum

Letter from a Parent

Dear Sir,
      I feel I ought to write
About Tom's essay-work last night.
Of all the subjects you have set
This seemed the most imprudent yet.
'Describe your family' . . . Tom did it,
So well, I just had to forbid it
Being handed in; – so did my wife.
The details of our family life
Are not of such a kind, alas,
That I should want them read in class:
We did not wish the High School staff
To scan them for a lunch-hour laugh.
We tore it out. I realize
You may think what we did unwise –
But give it your consideration
And please accept my explanation.
I trust you will not blame my son,
For, after all, the work *was done*.
          Yours truly
            Harold Honeybun

            Kenneth Kitchin

Blaming Sons

An Apology for his own Drunkenness (AD 406)

White hairs cover my temples.
I am wrinkled and gnarled beyond repair.
And though I have got five sons,
They all hate paper and brush.
A-shu is eighteen:
For laziness there is none like him.
A-hsüan does his best,
But really loathes the Fine Arts.
Yung and Tuan are thirteen,
But do not know 'six' from 'seven'.
T'ung-tzu in his ninth year
Is only concerned with things to eat.
If Heaven treats me like this,
What can I do but fill my cup?

T'ao Ch'ien
translated from the Chinese by
Arthur Waley

Parents' Evening

Tonight your mum and dad go off to school.
The classroom's empty.
Rabbit and gerbil sleep.
Your painting's with the others on the wall,
And all the projects you have ever done,
The long-since-finished and the just-begun,
Are ranged on desks.
Your books are in a pile.
'He gets fractions right,' your teacher says.
Your mother reads your 'news',
Is pleased to find you've prominently listed
The sticky pudding that you liked last Tuesday.

Suppose one evening you could go along
To see how mum and dad had spent their days,
What sort of work would you find up on show?
Bus-loads of people,
Towers of coins,
Letters to fill a hundred postmen's sacks,
Hayricks of dust from offices and houses,
Plates, cakes, trains, clothes,
Stretches of motorways and bridges,
Aeroplanes and bits of ships,
Bulldozers and paperclips,
'Cellos and pneumatic drills.
A noise to make the sleepy gerbil stir.

Shirley Toulson

The National Union of Children

NUC has just passed a weighty resolution:
'Unless all parents raise our rate of pay
This action will be taken by our members
(The resolution comes in force today):–

'Noses will not be blown (sniffs are in order),
Bedtime will get preposterously late,
Ice-cream and crisps will be consumed for breakfast,
Unwanted cabbage left upon the plate,

'Earholes and finger-nails can't be inspected,
Overtime (known as homework) won't be worked,
Reports from school will all say "Could do better",
Putting bricks back in boxes may be shirked.'

Roy Fuller

The National Association of Parents

Of course, N A P's answer quickly was forthcoming
(It was a matter of emergency),
It issued to the Press the following statement
(Its Secretary appeared upon TV):–

'True that the so-called Saturday allowance
Hasn't kept pace with prices in the shops,
But neither have, alas, parental wages;
N U C's claim would ruin kind, hard-working pops.

'Therefore, unless that claim is now abandoned,
Strike action for us, too, is what remains;
In planning for the which we are in process
Of issuing, to all our members, canes.'

Roy Fuller

Speech Day

The girls of the County Mod
are taught to believe in God,
team spirit, examination,
and the value of education.

Today, when speeches are made,
the usual things are said
to promote in the children zest
for what their elders think best.

As always, Alderman Mason,
on this auspicious occasion,
sums up with his proclamation:
'There's nowt like a good ejoocaashun.'

As the headmistress rises
and the girls go up for their prizes,
one wonders what Time will do
to this hopeful retinue –

these pink-cheeked dears who stand
glimpsing the promising land,
life like a motor-boat humming
and Christmas undoubtedly coming.

At type-writer, loom or till
most of these lasses will
mark time until they're wed.
Jane in a year will be dead.

Sally is destined to be
unmarried mother of three.
Only Rose, of the shining lights,
will attain the topmost heights.

Even Rose will sometimes ask,
at her magisterial desk
in another class-room, 'Mason,
were you right about education?'

May envy the never-dids
who graduate through palais,
coffee bar, bowling alley,
to husband, home, kids.

Francis Newbold

The Choosing

We were first equal Mary and I
with the same coloured ribbons in mouse-coloured hair,
and with equal shyness
we curtseyed to the lady councillor
for copies of Collins' Children's Classics.
First equal, equally proud.

Best friends too Mary and I
a common bond in being cleverest (equal)
in our small school's small class.
I remember
the competition for top desk
or to read aloud the lesson
at school service.
And my terrible fear
of her superiority at sums.

I remember the housing scheme
Where we both stayed.
The same house, different homes,
where the choices were made.

I don't know exactly why they moved,
but anyway they went.
Something about a three-apartment
and a cheaper rent.
But from the top deck of the high-school bus
I'd glimpse among the others on the corner
Mary's father, mufflered, contrasting strangely
with the elegant greyhounds by his side.

He didn't believe in high-school education,
especially for girls,
or in forking out for uniforms.

Ten years later on a Saturday –
I am coming home from the library –
sitting near me on the bus,
Mary
with a husband who is tall,
curly-haired, has eyes
for no one else but Mary.
Her arms are round the full-shaped vase
that is her body.
Oh, you can see where the attraction lies
in Mary's life –
not that I envy her, really.

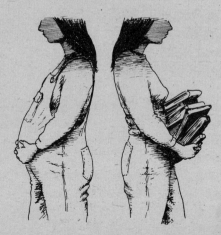

And I am coming from the library
with my arms full of books.
I think of the prizes that were ours for the taking
and wonder when the choices got made
we don't remember making.

Liz Lochhead

Thug

School began it.
There he felt
the tongue's salt lash
raising its welt

on a child's heart.
Ten years ruled
by violence left him
thoroughly schooled,

nor did he fail
to understand
the blow of the
headmaster's hand.

That hand his hand
round the cosh curled.
What rules the classroom
rocks the world.

Raymond Garlick

Oh Bring Back Higher Standards

Oh bring back higher standards –
the pencil and the cane –
if we want education then we must have some pain.
Oh, bring us back all the gone days
Yes, bring back all the past . . .
Yes, bring back all the past . . .
let's put them all in rows again – so we can see who's last.
Let's label all the good ones
(the ones like you and me)
and make them into prefects – like prefects used to be.
We'll put them on the honours board
. . . as honours ought to be,
and write their names in burnished script –
for all the world to see.
We'll have them back in uniform,
we'll have them doff their caps,
and learn what manners really are
. . . for decent kind of chaps!
. . . So let's label all the good ones,
we'll call them 'A's and 'B's –
and we'll parcel up the useless ones
and call them 'C's and 'D's.
. . . We'll even have an 'E' lot!
. . . an 'F' or 'G' maybe!!
. . . so they can know they're useless,
. . . and not as good as me.

For we've got to have the stupid –
And we've got to have the poor
Because –
        if we don't have them . . .
        well . . . what are prefects for?

Peter Dixon

School Report

'*Too easily satisfied. Spelling still poor.*
    Her grammar's erratic. Lacks care.
Would succeed if she worked. Inclined to be smug.'
    I think that's a wee bit unfare.

Ah well, their it is! Disappointing perhaps,
    For a mum what has always had brane,
But we can't all have looks or be good at our books . . .
    She's her father all over agane.

                                        Carole Paine

With Every Regret

For many years the undersigned
Has struggled to improve his mind;
He now is mortified and moved
To find it is not much improved.

His unremitting efforts were
To build a sterling character;
The best that he can really claim
Is that it is about the same.

He went through many a tedious drill
Developing the power of will,
The muscles, and the memory.
They're roughly what they used to be.

Alas! the inference is plain
That Education is in vain,
And all the end of our endeavour
Is to be just as dumb as ever.

Morris Bishop

I Remember, I Remember

I remember, I remember,
    The day that I left school;
It seemed to me that I was primed
    With knowledge to the full.
Ah me, 'twas childish ignorance,
    But now 'tis little joy
To know I'm rather more a dunce
    Than when I was a boy!

A. L. Haydon

Vitaï Lampada

There's a breathless hush in the Close tonight –
   Ten to make and the match to win –
A bumping pitch and a blinding light,
   An hour to play and the last man in.
And it's not for the sake of a ribboned coat,
   Or the selfish hope of a season's fame,
But his Captain's hand on his shoulder smote –
   'Play up! play up! and play the game!'

The sand of the desert is sodden red, –
   Red with the wreck of a square that broke; –
The Gatling's jammed and the Colonel dead,
   And the regiment blind with dust and smoke.
The river of death has brimmed his banks,
   And England's far, and Honour a name,
But the voice of a schoolboy rallies the ranks:
   'Play up! play up! and play the game!'

This is the word that year by year,
   While in her place the School is set,
Every one of her sons must hear,
   And none that hears it dare forget.
This they all with a joyful mind
   Bear through life like a torch in flame,
And falling fling to the host behind –
   'Play up! play up! and play the game!'

Henry Newbolt

Forty Years On

Forty years on, when afar and asunder,
   Parted are those who are singing today,
When you look back, and forgetfully wonder,
   What you were like in your work and your play;
Then, it may be, there will often come o'er you
   Glimpses of notes like the catch of a song –
Visions of boyhood shall float them before you,
   Echoes of dreamland shall bear them along.
      Follow up! follow up! follow up! follow up!
      Till the field ring again and again,
      With the tramp of the twenty-two men,
      Follow up! follow up!

*

O the great days, in the distance enchanted,
   Days of fresh air, in the rain and the sun,
How we rejoiced as we struggled and panted –
   Hardly believable, forty years on!
How we discoursed of them, one with another,
   Auguring triumph, or balancing fate,
Loved the ally with the heart of a brother,
   Hated the foe with a playing at hate!
      Follow up! follow up!

Forty years on, growing older and older,
    Shorter in wind and in memory long,
Feeble of foot and rheumatic of shoulder,
    What will it help you that once you were strong?
God gives us bases to guard or beleaguer,
    Games to play out, whether earnest or fun,
Fights for the fearless, and goals for the eager,
    Twenty, and thirty, and forty years on!
        Follow up! follow up!

Edward Ernest Bowen

The One Furrow

When I was young, I went to school
With pencil and foot-rule
Sponge and slate,
And sat on a tall stool
At learning's gate.

When I was older, the gate swung wide;
Clever and keen-eyed
In I pressed,
But found in the mind's pride
No peace, no rest.

Then who was it taught me back to go
To cattle and barrow,
Field and plough;
To keep to the one furrow,
As I do now?

R. S. Thomas

The Closed School

Under the silvering light of the cold, tall sky,
Where the stars are like glimmering ice and the moon
   rides high,
Bolted and locked since the war by long-dead hands,
Next to the shadowy church, the closed school stands.

A village school, in the grip of frost and the past,
Its classrooms airless as tombs, its corridors waste;
Behind boarded windows barely an insect crawls
On the spreading atlas that is staining ceilings and walls.

Here is the stillness of death. Listen hard as you can,
There's not one sound to be heard that is noisier than
The creeping of mould, or the crumbling of masonry
Into a fine floor-dust, soft and powdery.

Only deeper than silence, at the far end of listening,
Come the feet in the corridors, silver voices that ring
In the raftered hall, and outside, where the frost
    freezes hard,
Brittle laughter of children snowballing in the yard.

Raymond Wilson

At School-Close

The end has come, as come it must
    To all things; in these sweet June days
The teacher and the scholar trust
    Their parting feet to separate ways.

They part: but in the years to be
    Shall pleasant memories cling to each,
As shells bear inland from the sea
    The murmur of the rhythmic beach. . .

John Greenleaf Whittier

Index of First Lines

Index of Authors

Acknowledgements

The editor and publishers gratefully acknowledge permission to reproduce copyright poems in this book:

'Upright' by Ada Aharoni, reprinted by permission of the author; 'Dog in the Playground' by Allan Ahlberg from *Please Mrs Butler* by Allan Ahlberg (Kestrel Books), copyright © 1983 by Allan Ahlberg, reprinted by permission of Penguin Books Ltd; 'Duty of the Student' and 'Character Building' by Edward Anthony, copyright © 1947, 1975 by Watson-Guptill Publications, Inc., reprinted by permission of Watson-Guptill Publications, Inc.; 'The Nature Lesson' by Marjorie Baldwin, reprinted from *The Slain Unicorn* by permission of the author; two extracts from *Summoned by Bells* by John Betjeman, reprinted by permission of John Murray (Publishers) Ltd; 'With Every Regret' by Morris Bishop, reprinted from *Children's Book of Comic Verse* by permission of Batsford Ltd; 'The Crib' by Guy Boas, reprinted from *Lays of Learning* by permission of Hutchinson Ltd; 'Animal Chatter' by Gyles Brandreth, reprinted by permission of the author; 'Listen While You Speak' and 'My Son Asks Me' by Bertolt Brecht, reprinted from *Brecht's Poems* by permission of Associated Book Publishers Ltd; 'The Chemistry Hour' by Gerald Bullett, reprinted from *Collected Poems* by permission of J. M. Dent & Sons Ltd; 'Timothy Winters' by Charles Causley, reprinted by permission of the author from *Collected Poems*, published by Macmillan; 'A Day in the Country' and 'Dunce' by Leonard Clark, reprinted from *The Corn Growing* by permission of Hodder & Stoughton Ltd; 'Odd-Job Boy', 'A Boy Left Over', 'A Rolling Stone', 'In the Playground' and 'School in the Holidays' by Stanley Cook, reprinted by permission of the author; 'School's Out' by W. H. Davies, reprinted from *The Complete Poems of W. H. Davies* by permission of the Executors of the W. H. Davies Estate and of Jonathan Cape Ltd; 'The Dunce' and 'The Bookworm' by Walter de la Mare, reprinted by permission of the Literary Trustees of Walter de la Mare and the Society of Authors as their representative; 'Patterns' by Olive Dehn, reprinted by permission of the author; 'King of the Toilets' and 'Oh Bring Back Higher Standards' by Peter Dixon, reprinted by permission of the author; 'Blackboard Jungle' by Julian Ennis, reprinted by permission of Newnes Books; 'Arithmetic' by Gavin Ewart, reprinted from *The Deceptive Grin of the Gravel Porters* (London

Magazine Editions) by permission of the author; 'Schoolbell' by Eleanor Farjeon, reprinted from *The Children's Bells* (Oxford University Press) by permission of David Higham Associates Ltd; 'Visit to a Graveyard' and 'Friday' by Eric Finney, reprinted by permission of the author; 'Epitaph', 'The National Union of Children' and 'The National Association of Parents' by Roy Fuller, reprinted from *Seen Grandpa Lately?* (1972) by permission of André Deutsch Ltd; 'Thug' by Raymond Garlick, reprinted from *Incense* by permission of the author and of Gwasg Gomer, Llandysul; 'Geography Lesson' by Zulfikar Ghose, reprinted from *Jets of Orange* by permission of Macmillan, London and Basingstoke; 'Distracted the Mother Said to Her Boy' by Gregory Harrison, from *A Fourth Poetry Book*, compiled by John Foster (Oxford University Press, 1982), reprinted by permission of Gregory Harrison; 'Mid-Term Break' by Seamus Heaney, reprinted from *Death of a Naturalist* by permission of Faber & Faber; 'Sally' by Phoebe Hesketh, reprinted from *Song of Sunlight*, by permission of The Bodley Head; 'The Place's Fault' by Philip Hobsbaum, reprinted by permission of the author; 'The Lover' by Julie Holder, from *The Third Poetry Book*, compiled by John Foster (Oxford University Press, 1982), reprinted by permission of Julie Holder; 'A History Lesson' by Miroslav Holub from *Miroslav Holub: Selected Poems*, trans. Ian Milner and George Theiner (Penguin Modern European Poets), copyright © Miroslav Holub, 1967, translation copyright © Penguin Books Ltd, 1967, reprinted by permission of Penguin Books Ltd; 'I'm a Treble in the Choir' by Edmond Kapp, reprinted from *Children's Book of Comic Verse* by permission of Batsford Ltd; 'Teachers' Features', 'Sense of Vocation', 'Letter from a Parent', 'Lock Up Your Javelins' by Kenneth Kitchin, reprinted by permission of Gerald Duckworth & Co. Ltd; 'The Best of School' by D. H. Lawrence, reprinted by permission of Laurence Pollinger Ltd, and the Estate of Mrs Frieda Lawrence Ravagli; 'The Choosing' by Liz Lochhead, reprinted by permission of the author; 'The Lesson' by Edward Lucie-Smith, reprinted by permission of the author; 'The Lesson', 'He Who Owns the Whistle Rules the World', 'Nooligan' and 'Streemin' by Roger McGough, reprinted from *In the Classroom* by permission of the author and of Jonathan Cape Ltd; 'The School Field in December' and 'A Hot Day at the School' by Wes Magee, reprinted by permission of the author; 'If the Teacher was a Robot' by Paul Marsh, reprinted by permission of the Hamlyn Publishing Group; 'For a Junior School Poetry Book' by Christopher Middleton, reprinted by permission of the author from

111 Poems, published by Carcanet Press; 'The ABC' by Spike Milligan, reprinted by permission of the author; 'Dumb Insolence' by Adrian Mitchell, reprinted by permission of the author and Allison & Busby Ltd; 'Holiday Here Today' by Julian Mitchell, reprinted by permission of Cadbury Ltd; 'To David, about his Education' by Howard Nemerov, reprinted from *The Collected Poems of Howard Nemerov* (University of Chicago Press, 1977) by permission of the author; 'Vitai Lampada' by Henry Newbolt, reprinted by permission of Peter Newbolt; 'Wild Flowers' by Peter Newell, reprinted by permission of Harper & Row; 'The Pain' and 'Skipping Song' by Gareth Owen, reprinted by permission of Fontana Paperbacks; 'Our School', 'Friday Morning Last Two Lessons is Games Day' and 'Winter' by Gareth Owen, reprinted by permission of the author from *Salford Road* (obtainable from the author); 'School Report' by Carole Paine, reprinted by permission of Punch Publications Ltd; 'A Page of Handwriting' by Jacques Prévert, reprinted by permission of Gallimard and of the translator, Keith Bosley; 'Olympic Special' and 'Rodge Said' by Michael Rosen, copyright © Michael Rosen, 1979, reprinted from *You Tell Me* by Roger McGough and Michael Rosen (Kestrel Books), by permission of Penguin Books Ltd; 'Arithmetic' by Carl Sandburg from *The Complete Poems of Carl Sandburg*, copyright 1950 by Carl Sandburg, renewed 1978 by Margaret Sandburg, Helga Sandburg Crile and Janet Sandburg, reprinted by permission of Harcourt Brace Jovanovich, Inc.; 'Conkers' by Clive Sansom, reprinted by permission of the author; 'Growing Pain' by Vernon Scannell, reprinted by permission of the author; 'Homework Machine' by Shel Silverstein, reprinted from *A Light in the Attic* by permission of the author and of Jonathan Cape Ltd; 'Out of School' by Hal Summers, © Hal Summers, 1978. Reprinted from *Tomorrow is My Love* by Hal Summers (1978), by permission of Oxford University Press; 'Blaming Sons' by T'ao Ch'ien, translated by Arthur Waley, reprinted from *Chinese Poems*, by permission of Allen & Unwin Ltd; 'Bird in the Classroom' by Colin Thiele, reprinted by permission of the author; 'The One Furrow' by R. S. Thomas, reprinted from *Song at the Year's Turning* by permission of Granada Publishing Ltd; 'Romance' by W. J. Turner, reprinted by permission of Sidgwick & Jackson Ltd; 'A Lapp at School in Finland' by Nils-Aslak Valkeapää, reprinted by permission of the author and of the translators, Hannele Branch and Keith Bosley; 'I've Got an Apple Ready', 'The Bully Asleep', 'Bus to School' and 'Bus Home' by John Walsh, reprinted from *The Roundabout by the Sea*, by John